Excel

BASIC SKILLS

COMPUTING SKILLS
Years 1–2

Tim Tuck

ISBN 1 74020 284 8

Pascal Press
PO Box 250
Glebe NSW 2037
(02) 8585 4044
www.pascalpress.com.au

Publisher: Vivienne Petris Joannou
Edited by Shelley Barons and Fiona Sim
Typeset by Tim Tuck
Cover by DiZign
Illustrations by Vicki Earles
Printed in Australia by Printing Creations

Dedication
To my own two 'bots, Emma and Sarah.

Contents

To the Parent or Teacher

Computers are now almost standard fixtures in classrooms and homes and children often know more about their operation than the adults do!

But sometimes that knowledge may go little further than knowing how to start the computer and run a few favourite games or programs. The computer is a complex and multi-faceted tool and students are being required to use word processors, spreadsheets, databases, graphic programs and Internet research in the daily course of their studies.

This book, written for Microsoft® Windows for PC, aims to introduce children to those applications in a sequenced program of work units. The book begins with an introduction to three characters who will offer help and guidance (and some amusement!) throughout the different units. When the student completes the exercises and activities in this book he or she will have been exposed to a variety of computer processes and programs and will have practised a variety of skills.

Some points to note:

- There is no set pathway through the material. Units may be taken out of sequence; just be aware that work within a unit often builds on previously taught skills.
- Keyboarding skills are integral to nearly all activities on the computer. To achieve a useful typing speed children will need regular practice and a range of additional exercises outside of the scope of this book. Consider investing in a good touch-typing program or use one of the many free online courses.
- Encourage children to experiment with the various tools and programs but establish rules about what they can—and can't—change. This may include such things as the Desktop colours and wallpaper.
- The Microsoft® Office word processor 'Word' may be used instead of WordPad as the commands and processes are almost identical.

Level of difficulty

The activities and projects in this book are aimed at older year 1s and 2s. Some of the activities are more difficult as a challenge for more able students. Some younger children may need help with reading the accompanying text.

Activities

Most pages have a 'Questions' section. These are usually answered on the page from the information supplied or from viewing a computer screen.

The 'Your turn' sections are short exercises to be completed using the suggested program.

Requirements

- A personal computer running Windows 95, 98 or 2000.
- A printer.
- Connection to the Internet. (Required for Unit 6.)
- The programs used for exercises in this book (WordPad, Paint, Internet Explorer and Outlook Express) are usually installed as part of Windows.

Note that computers are not all set up identically, so some screenshots of programs, menus and folders in the book may differ from your own computer.

1. Cross out the letters p-e-w-t-a to discover Pewta's favourite animal.

p	s	e	e	w	a	t	a	s	l

2. Cross out the letters m-o-u-s-e-b-o-t to discover Mouse-bot's favourite food.

m	c	o	u	h	s	e	e	e	s	b	e	o	t

3. Cross out the letters f-l-o-p-p-y-b-o-t to discover Floppy-bot's favourite book.

f	l	d	o	i	c	p	t	i	p	o	p	n	y	b	a	o	r	t	y

What Box is What?

Questions

1. Read each sentence. Find the picture of the part and write its name in the box.

Keyboard
A flat board with letter and number keys.

Mouse
A small round-shaped object with buttons.

System box
A large box with power lights and slots.

Printer
A box that prints out on paper stored inside.

Monitor
A screen that connects to the computer.

Speakers
Two boxes that play music and sound.

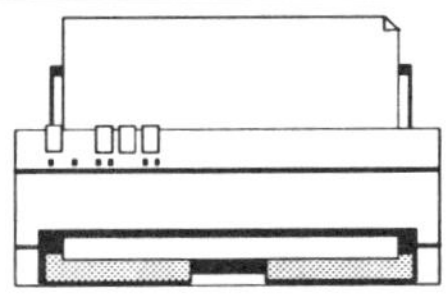	a.
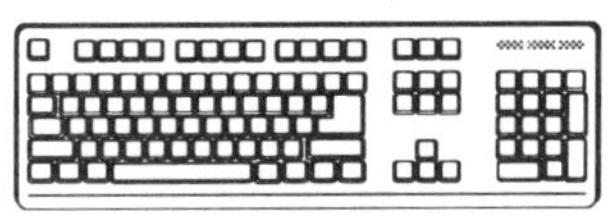	b.
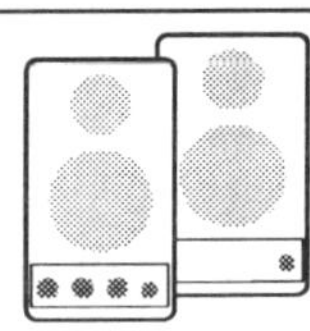	c.
	d.
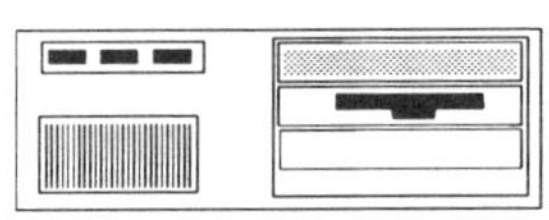	e.
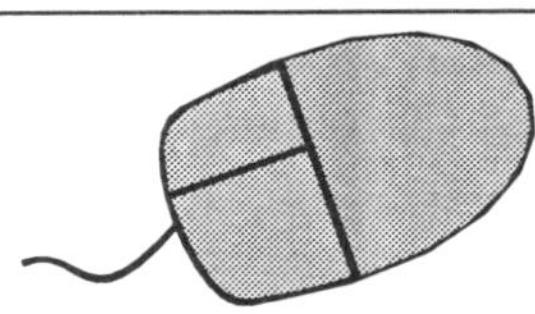	f.

2. Pewta has made signs to hang on her computer but she's jumbled up the letters. Write the correct word underneath each one.

a. parkeess   b. tonimor   c. bydorake   d. messyt xob   e. tripern

________   ________   ________   ________   ________

Buttons, Buttons Everywhere

Your computer's **power button** turns it on and off.
The **reset button** restarts your computer if it crashes or stops.
The **CD drive eject button** and **floppy disk drive eject button** push disks out.

Questions

1. Draw your system box buttons in the spaces below.

power	reset	CD drive eject	floppy disk drive

2. Pewta found some other buttons and keys. How many of them can you find? Tick each one as you find it. Write their names in the spaces.

a. 

____________________ ☐

b. 

____________________ ☐

c. 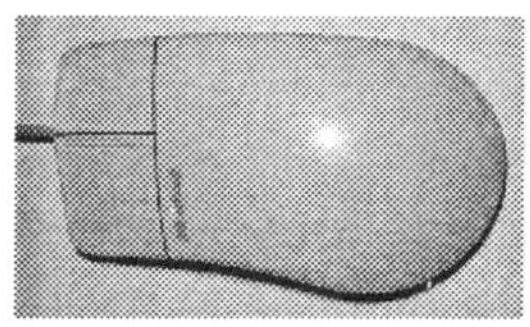

____________________ ☐

d. 

____________________ ☐

e. 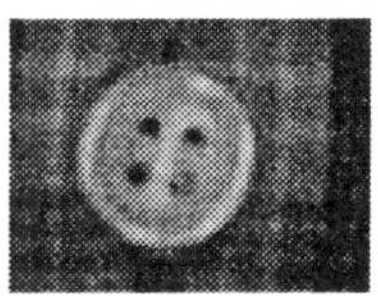

____________________ ☐

f. 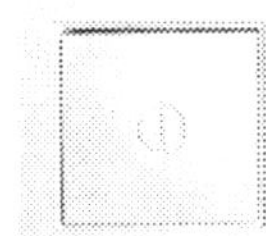

____________________ ☐

shirt button
arrow keys
Windows key
mouse buttons
monitor button
backspace key

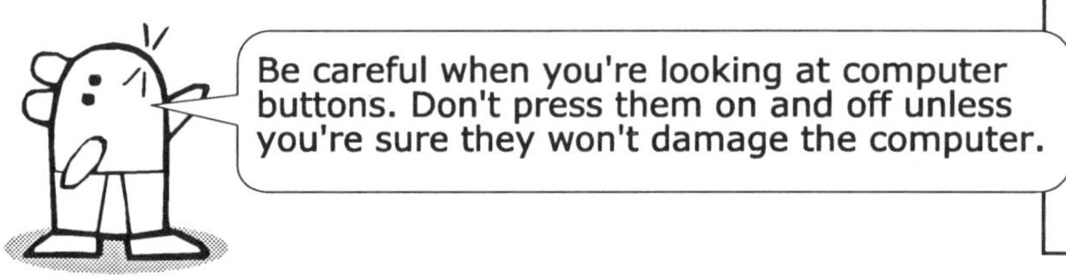

CD-ROMs and Floppy Disks

Pewta's favourite computer game came on a shiny disk called a **CD-ROM**. Sometimes she saves her stories on a square plastic **floppy disk**.

Questions

1. Write the name of these disks.

a. ____________

b. ________________________

2. Read the clues below. Is the clue about a CD-ROM or a floppy disk? Colour in the box to show your answer.

a. Has a surface like a mirror.
b. Has a sliding metal window.
c. Stores information.
d. Is almost a square.
e. Is a circle.
f. Has a disk inside.

CD-ROM	floppy disk
CD-ROM	floppy disk
CD-ROM	floppy disk
CD-ROM	floppy disk
CD-ROM	floppy disk
CD-ROM	floppy disk

3. Pewta's favourite computer game is called 'Sammy the Seal's Big Adventure'. What is your favourite computer game? Write its name here:

____

Draw its picture on the disk.

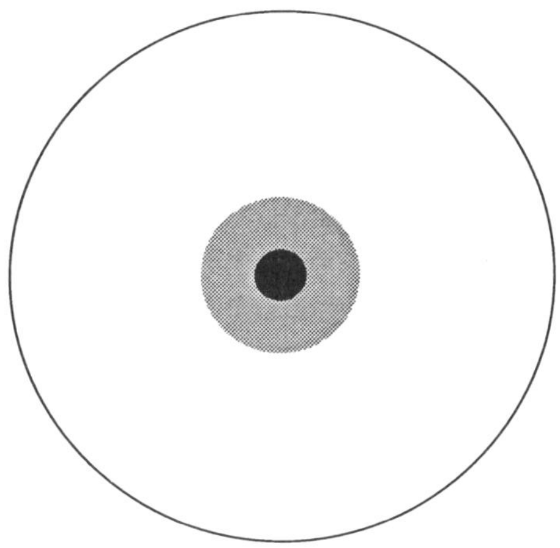

Taking Care of Your Disks

Pewta dropped her 'Sammy the Seal' CD-ROM game on the floor. Mouse-bot accidentally stepped on it. Now it doesn't work properly.

Questions

1. Which of these rules would help Pewta care for her CD-ROMs?

   Tick the true ones.

   a. Put CD-ROMs away in their covers when you finish. ☐
   b. Don't leave CD-ROMs in the car on hot days. ☐
   c. Keep CD-ROMs piled on top of your computer. ☐
   d. Use your good CD-ROMs as drink mats. ☐
   e. Place CD-ROMs carefully into the drive. ☐
   f. It's okay to use CD-ROMs as frisbees. ☐
   g. Try to pick up CD-ROMs by the edges. ☐

2. Pewta found these drawings on a box of floppy disks. What do you think each one means? Use these words:

magnets	hot	closed	disk

   Write your answers below the pictures.

a. Don't touch the	b. Keep the cover	c. Keep away from	d. Don't let disks get too

Keeping Safe and Healthy

Make a list of rules for your computer. Check with your parents or teacher to see if there are any special rules you need to include.

Questions

1. Read these rules.
   Which keep you safe and healthy?
   Which keep your computer safe and healthy?
   Tick the best box.

   a. Keep food and drink away from the computer. ☐ me ☐ computer

   b. Keep the computer desk clean and tidy. ☐ me ☐ computer

   c. Be gentle with the keyboard and other hardware. ☐ me ☐ computer

   d. Turn the computer off properly when you finish. ☐ me ☐ computer

   e. Remember to take a break every now and then. ☐ me ☐ computer

   f. Share the computer with other people. ☐ me ☐ computer

2. Here's Pewta working at her computer. But she isn't quite following all the rules! Write the letter of the rule she's breaking next to the arrow.

Let's get Started...

To start her home computer Pewta:

1. Pushes the power button.
2. Waits for Windows to appear.

When Pewta is at school she:

1. Pushes the power button.
2. Types in her name and password.

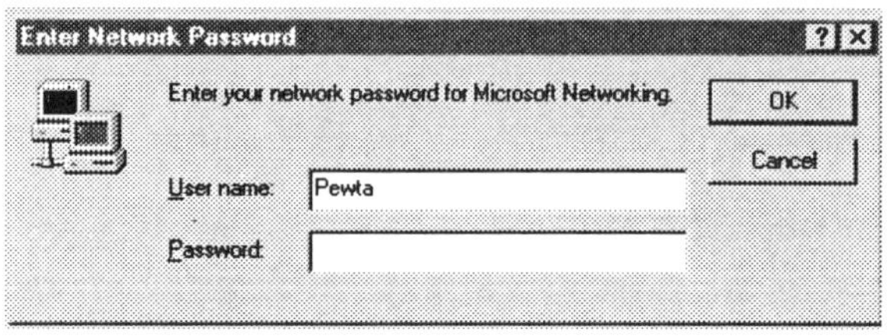

3. Clicks **OK**.
4. Waits for Windows to appear.

Some computers are used by lots of different people. They use different programs and files. After pressing the power button they **log in**. This tells the computer who they are.

Question

What do you do to start Windows? Write each of the steps below.

Let's get Finished

Don't just press the power button off when you finish on the computer.

To turn the computer off

1. Click the **Start** button.
2. Click **Shut Down**...
3. Click the **Shut Down** radio button.
4. Click **OK**.

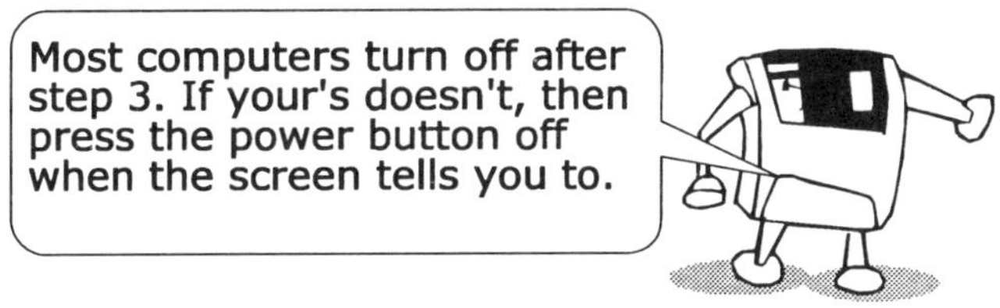

Questions

1. Which step did you see each of these pictures in?
   Write a number in the box.

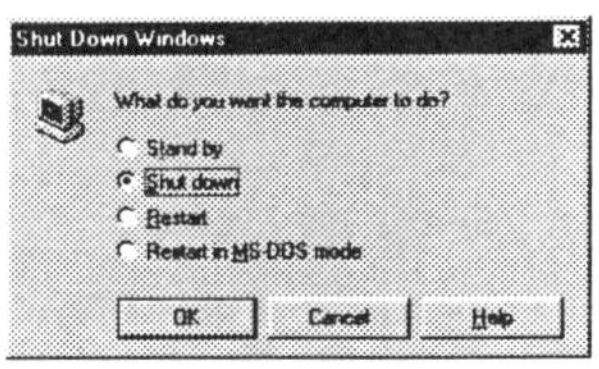

a. ☐ b. ☐ c. ☐

2. At school, Pewta doesn't turn the computer off.
   Instead, she has to **log off**.
   This tells the computer she's finished using it.
   If you have to log off, put these steps in order.

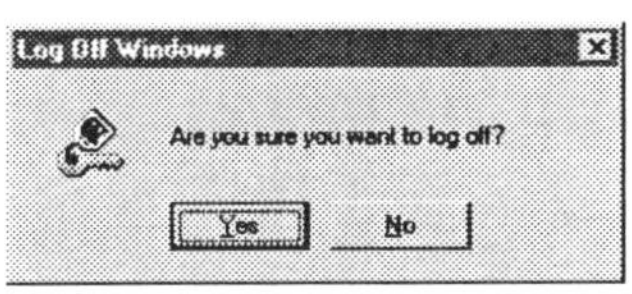

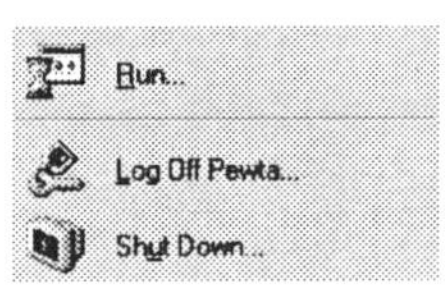

a. ☐ b. ☐ c. ☐

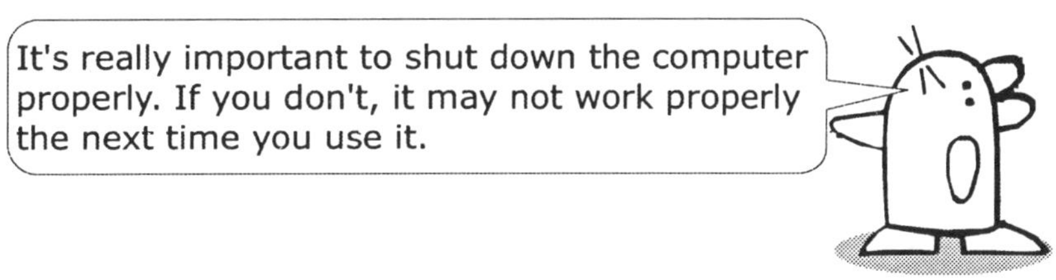

The Desktop

Here's Pewta drawing at her desk. She doesn't keep it very tidy does she!

See if you can find her:

pencil case	☐	story writing book	☐
calculator	☐	drawing pad	☐
lollies	☐	sandwich	☐

When Pewta starts her computer, this is what she sees. It's called the desktop. It's much tidier than her real desk!

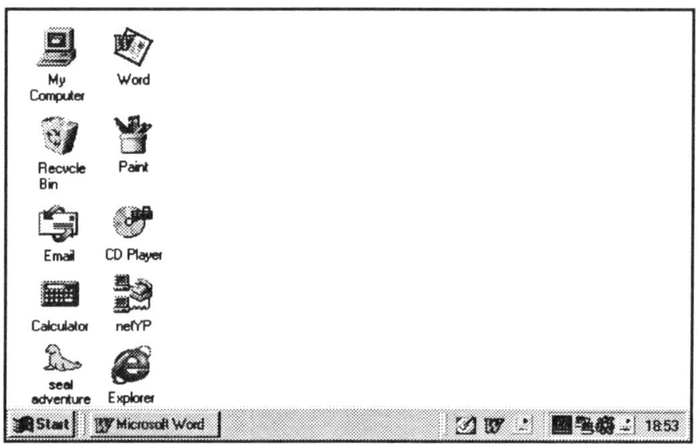

The desktop has small pictures called icons on it. Each icon starts a different computer program. Tick each box as you find the icon for:

Her paint program	☐	Her word processor	☐
Her calculator	☐	Her favourite game	☐
Her CD player	☐	Her email program	☐
The Recycle Bin	☐	The Start button	☐
The Clock	☐	My Computer	☐

Mouse Skills (1)

Questions

1. Label these pictures: computer mouse, Mouse-bot, real mouse

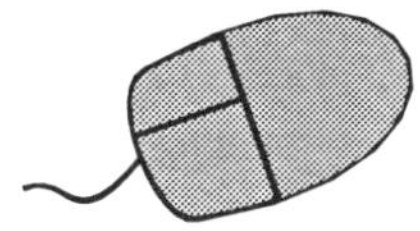

a.	b.	c.

2. Here's Pewta's computer mouse. It has two buttons.

   Draw your computer mouse in the box.

3. When you move your mouse, the pointer on the screen moves. Draw an arrow on each screen below to show where the mouse pointer moves. Write the direction in the box. Use the words right, down, up and left.

   a. Move the mouse **forward**

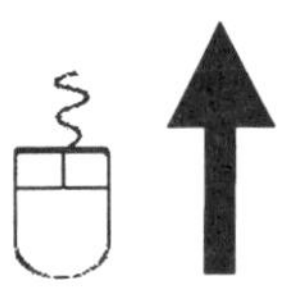
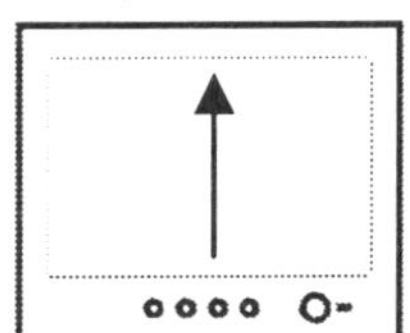

   b. Move the mouse **backward**

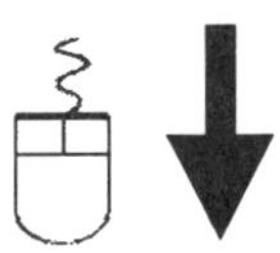

   c. Move the mouse **left**

   d. Move the mouse **right**

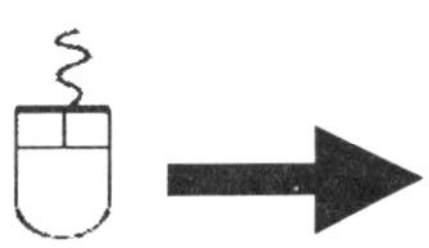
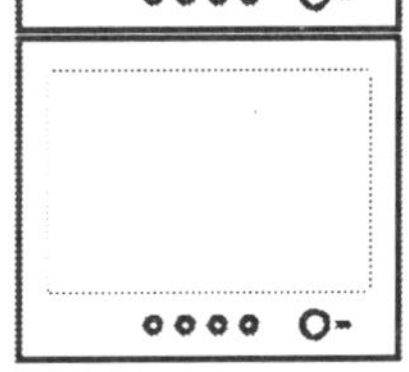

Mouse Skills (2)

Questions

1. Pewta can't always remember her left and right. Can you?
In each picture circle:

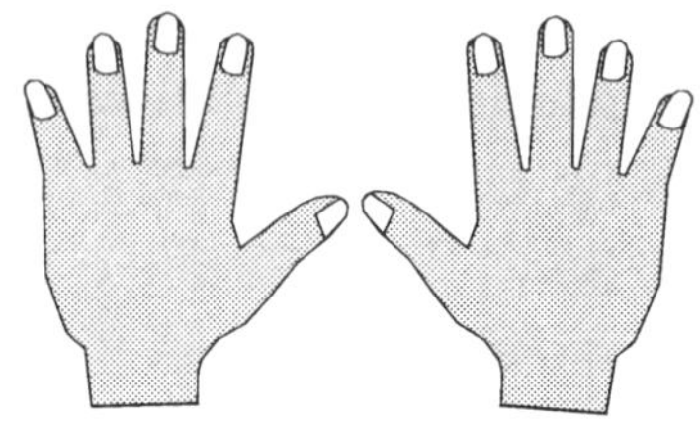

a. the left 'bot. b. the left key c. the left hand.

2. Label this mouse with right button and left button.

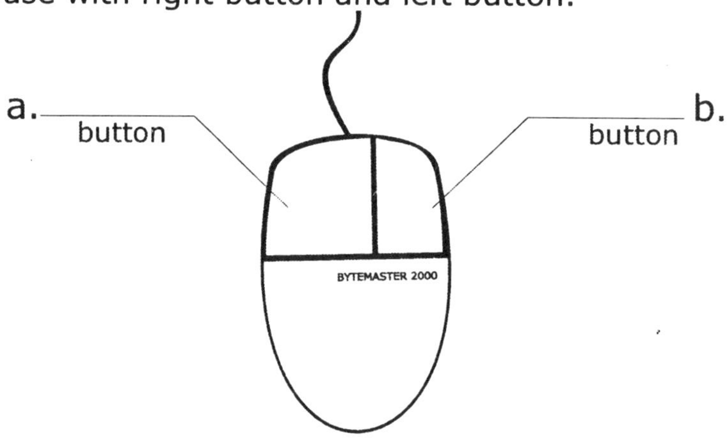

c. The __________ button is used the most. It's used for:

- starting programs
- selecting information
- moving objects around.

d. The __________ button isn't used as much. It's used for:

- making small menus appear next to an object
- selecting background colours in Paint.

3. Usually the pointer on your screen is an arrow. But sometimes the pointer changes. Pewta went looking for mouse pointers and found these.
Tick them off as you discover each one.

Mouse Skills (3)

There are four types of mouse-button clicking to learn.

Questions

1. Fill in the missing words. Use the words: right, drag, twice and left.

Left click 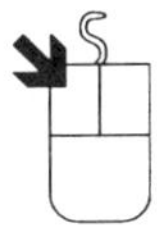

a. Tap the __________ button.

Double-clicking 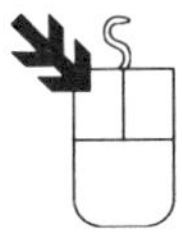

b. Quickly tap the left button _____________.

Click and drag 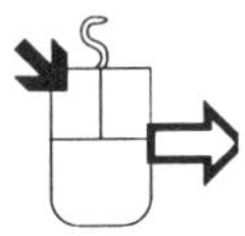

c. Press the left mouse button down.
_____________ the mouse.
Release the button.

Right click 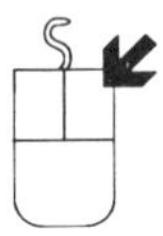

d. Tap the __________ button.

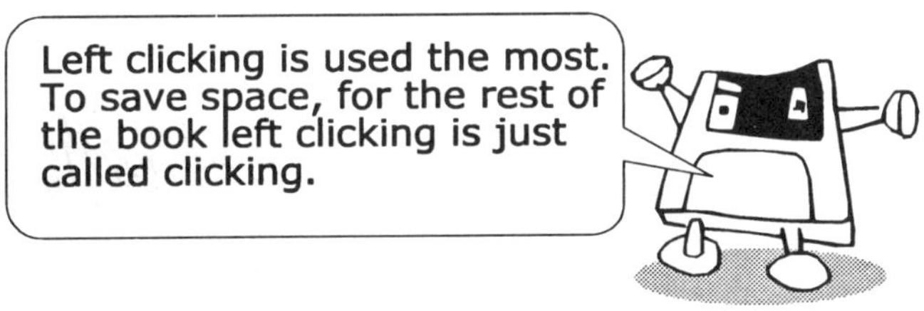

2. Find the **My Computer** icon on your desktop. 
Try each type of clicking in turn. Draw a line to match up the sentences.

a. Left click  — The My Computer program starts.

b. Click and drag  — A small menu appears.

c. Right click  — The My Computer icon changes colour.

d. Double-click  — The My Computer icon moves.

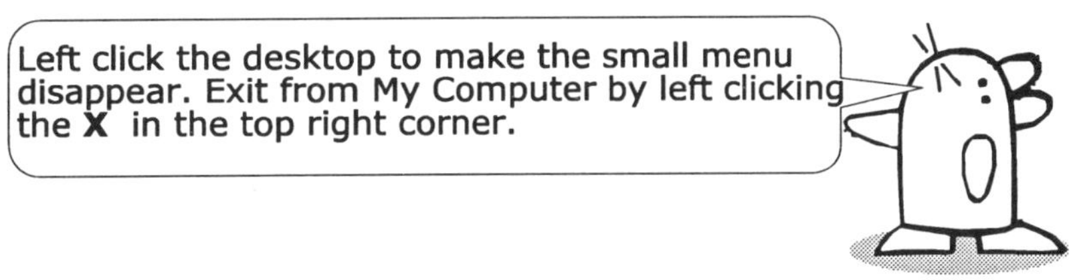

What's on the Menu?

A restaurant menu is a list of the meals ready to order—and eat!
Your computer has menus too. Computer menus are lists of programs to run or instructions to follow. The biggest menu on your computer is the Start menu. To see the start menu, click the **Start** button. 

Questions

1. The Start menu has eight choices at the bottom.
   Match the sentences below to the choice on the menu.
   Write the letter in the circle.

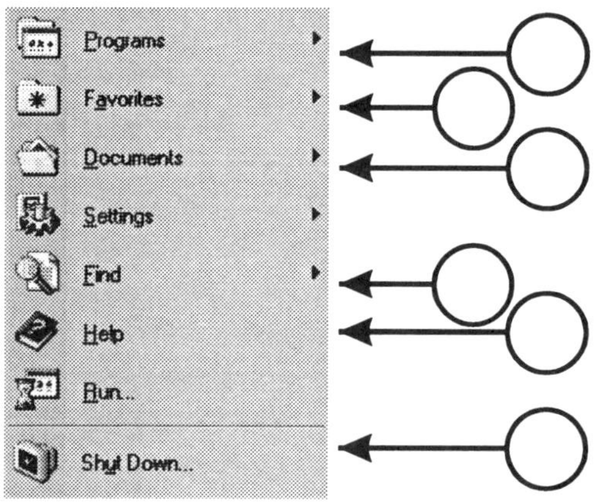

a. Choose your **favourite** programs and documents.
b. **Find** documents and programs.
c. Get **help** on using your computer.
d. **Shut down** your computer.
e. Open recent **documents**.
f. Use **programs** and games.

Did you notice the small arrow next to the five menu choices at the top? When you point to these choices a further menu appears. When Pewta points at her programs menu, this menu appears:

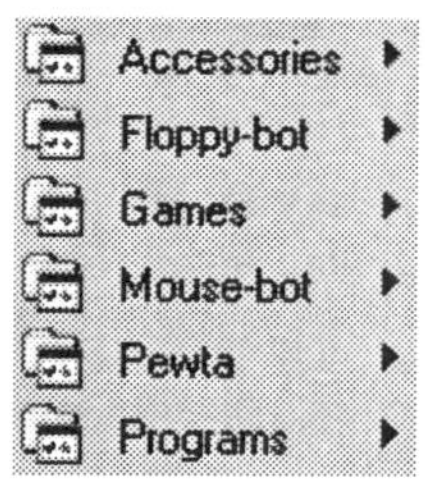

2. What do you see when you point to *your* program menu?

   Write some of your choices on this menu.

   Don't forget to include an arrow if there is one!

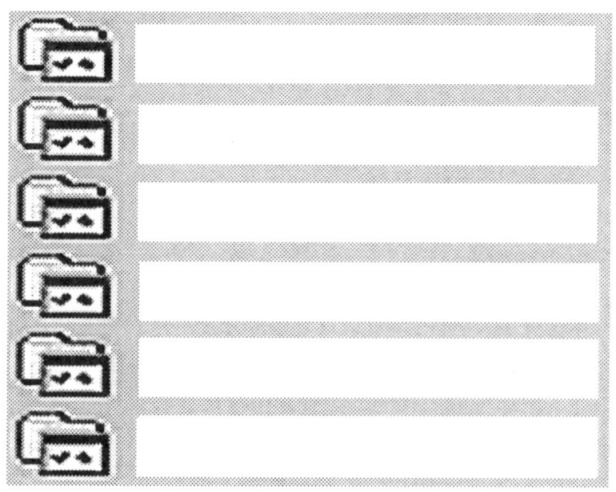

Opening and Closing Programs

You can start programs from the **Start menu** or from the **desktop**.
Tick off each step as you complete it.

Questions

To open a program from the desktop

1. Point to the program's icon.
2. Double-click the icon.

To open a program from the start menu

1. Click the **Start** button. Start
2. Point at **Programs**.
3. Point to the menu that has your program.
4. Click the program.

To close a program

Point at the ☒ in the top corner and click.

1. Write the name of another program on your desktop.

____

2. Write the name of a program you can open from your Start menu.

____

3. Do you a different way to close a program? Explain how.

____

____

Your Turn

Follow the instructions below. Tick each step as you complete it.

Open My Computer

Double-click **My Computer**. ☐

Close My Computer

Click the ☒ button. ☐

Open WordPad

1. Click **Start**.
2. Point at **Programs**. Programs ☐
3. Point at **Accessories**. Accessories ☐
4. Click **WordPad**. WordPad ☐

The Paint Screen

There are thousands of different Windows programs.
But they all have things that are the same, such as menus and toolbars.
Let's look at Paint, Windows' very own drawing and painting program.

To start Paint

1. Click **Start**.
2. Point at **Programs**.
3. Point at **Accessories**. 

4. Click **Paint**. 

While you've got Paint open, why don't you try some painting? Look at pages 57–64 for some ideas.

Questions

1. Here's the Paint screen. Label the parts of the screen. Use the words below.

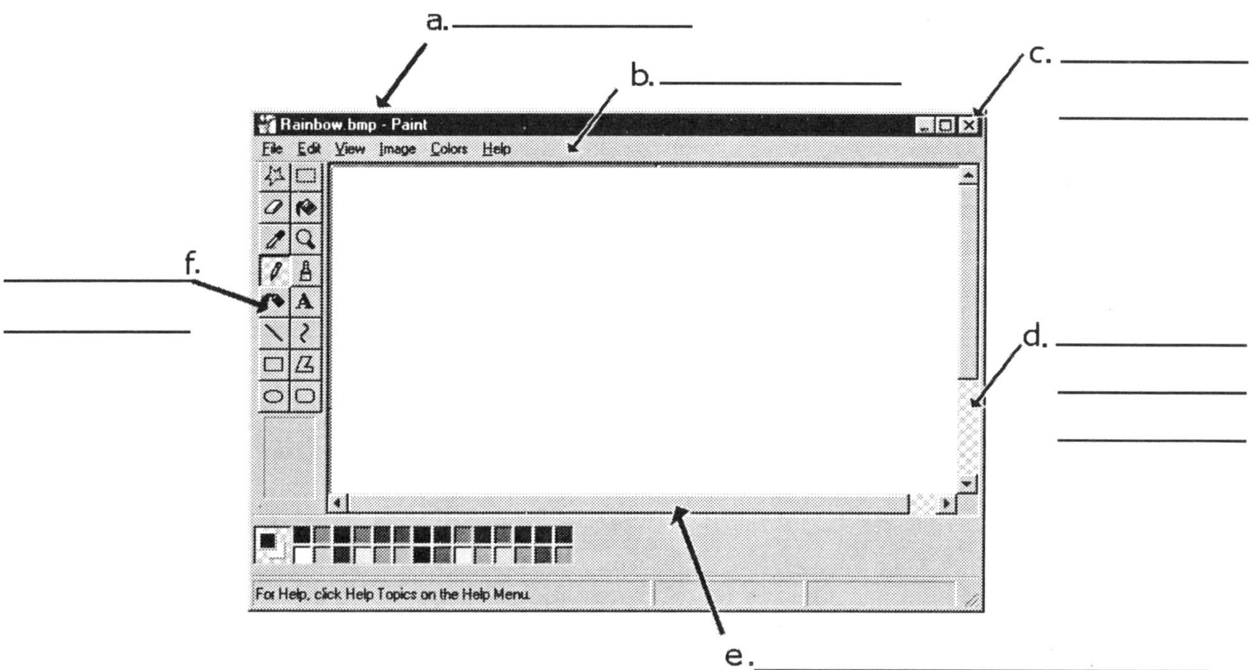

title bar

menu bar
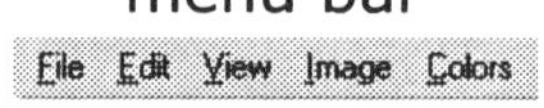

horizontal scroll bar
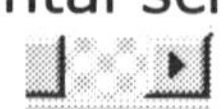

vertical scroll bar

tool bar
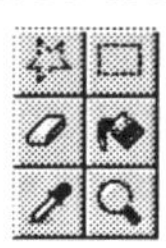

close button

The WordPad Screen

WordPad is Windows' word processing program.
WordPad's window has some of the same parts as the Paint window.

To start WordPad

1. Click **Start** and point at **Programs**.
2. Point at **Accessories**.
3. Click **WordPad**. 

Questions

1. Label the different parts of the screen using the labels below. Look back to page 16 for help. Use these words:

Close button	title bar	menu bar	tool bar	vertical scroll bar	horizontal scroll bar

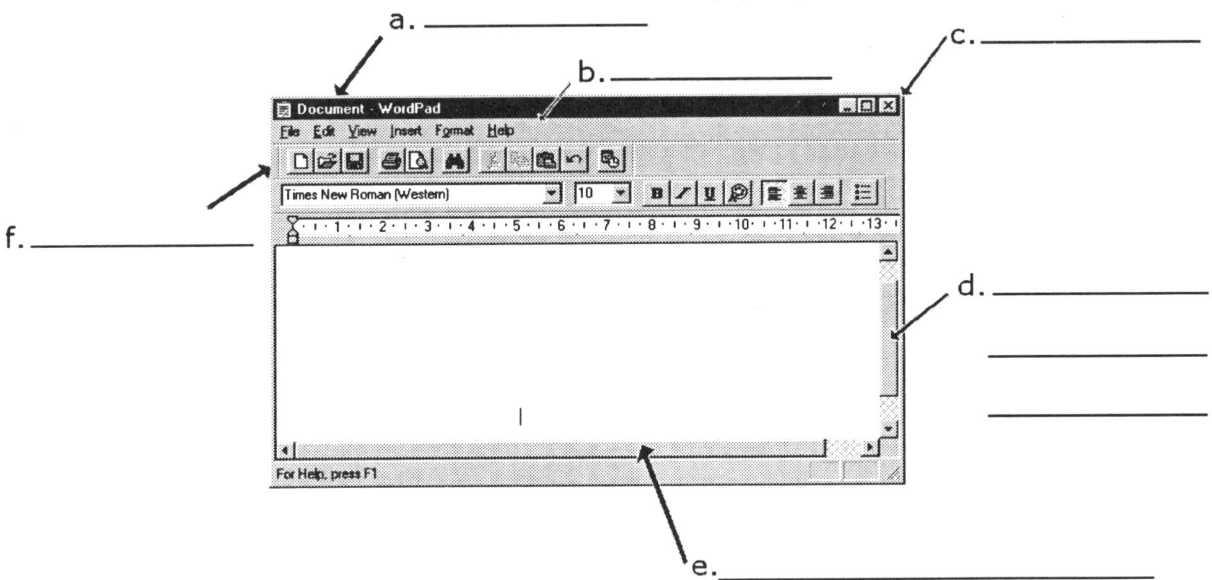

2. Tick the best answer to these questions.

   a. Click on the word **File** on the menu bar. What happens?
   A menu drops down ☐ The word changes colour ☐

   b. Double-click on the **title bar**. What happens?
   Nothing ☐ The window changes size ☐

   c. Point the mouse at the centre of the page. What happens?
   The pointer changes to I ☐ The pointer changes to  ☐

Taking Turns

Here are some reasons for sharing your computer.

- So my brothers or sisters can have a turn.
- So my parents can check their emails.
- Because I shouldn't be on the computer all day.
- So mum or dad can play their favourite game.

Questions

1. Write another reason why you should share your computer at home.

   ____

2. Write a reason why we share computers at school.

   ____

3. Who shares your computer?
   Write what they use it for. Write your name first.

Person	What they use the computer for

4. Look at Pewta's roster for sharing the computer.

   a. Is it fair or unfair? ____________Why? ________________________

   b. Write a roster for sharing your home or class computer.

Pewta's roster

Person	Day
Pewta	Mon.
Mouse-bot	Tue.
Pewta	Wed.
Floppy-bot	Thu.
Pewta	Fri.

Your roster

Person	Day
	Mon.
	Tue.
	Wed.
	Thu.
	Fri.

Caring for Yourself

Playing on the computer is fun.
But your body can get tired sitting in the same place for too long.
When you use the computer:

1. Take a break every hour or so.
2. When you take a break, stretch and get some fresh air.
3. Sit in the computer chair properly; don't slouch!
4. Use both hands on the keyboard.

Questions

Pewta's been playing computer games since 3 o'clock.
Mouse-bot took this photo of her.

1. Is Pewta sitting properly at the computer? Yes ☐ No ☐

2. Pewta has been playing games for
   a. One hour. ☐
   b. Two hours. ☐
   c. Three hours. ☐

3. What should Pewta do now? (tick one box)
   a. Play for longer. ☐
   b. Take a break. ☐
   c. Lean back in her chair. ☐

4. What else is Pewta doing wrong? ____________________

Who Owns What?

Stealing is taking something that doesn't belong to you.
Stealing from a shop isn't fair to the owners so it's against the law.
Programs, games, graphics and stories take a lot of time and hard work to make.
Copying programs without paying for them is stealing.
So is pretending someone else's work is yours.

Questions

1. Write an answer to these questions.

   a. It's wrong to steal from shops because it isn't ___________to the owners.

   b. Programs, games and graphics take lots of ____________ work to make.

   c. ______________ a program you haven't bought is called stealing.

   d. _____________ someone else's work is yours is also called stealing.

2. Pewta's drawn a picture on the computer. She likes her picture so much she prints it out. She hangs it on the fridge to look at.
   Colour the best answer. Can Mouse-bot:

a. Look at Pewta's picture?	Yes	No	Ask Pewta first
b. Make a copy of Pewta's picture?	Yes	No	Ask Pewta first
c. Pretend Pewta's picture is his?	Yes	No	Ask Pewta first

3. Do you think you can copy your own stories and pictures? Yes ☐ No ☐
4. How would you feel if someone copied a story you'd written and pretended it belonged to them? ____

   ____
5. Who wrote this book? ____

Welcome to WordPad

A word processor is a program for writing. Pewta uses her word processor to write stories, lists, labels and reports. The word processor has tools to help you:

edit

format

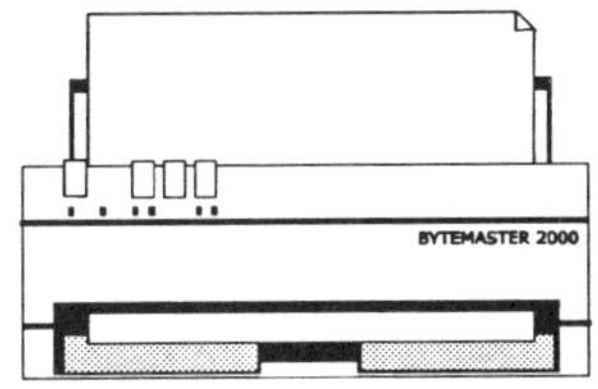

send text to a printer

Windows' word processor is called WordPad.
Follow the instructions on page 17 to start WordPad.

Special keys

Find these special keys on your computer keyboard. Tick each key as you find it.

- ☐ Backspace key
- ☐ Enter key
- ☐ Space bar

Your Turn

- Type your name onto the screen.
- Press the **space bar** to leave a space.
- Type your name again and leave a space (answer question 1).
- Press the **backspace key** a few times (answer question 2).
- Press the backspace key until you've erased all your names.
- Type your name again and press the **Enter key** once (answer question 3)

Questions

1. How many times did your name fit before it jumped to the next line?_________

2. What happens when you press **Backspace**? ____________________________

3. What happens when you press **Enter**? ________________________________

What's where in WordPad

Questions

1. Here's a picture of the WordPad screen. What is each arrow pointing to? Use this list of words to help you decide. Pages 16 and 17 might help too.

title bar	document window	menu bar	ruler
tool bar	close button	vertical scroll bar	file menu

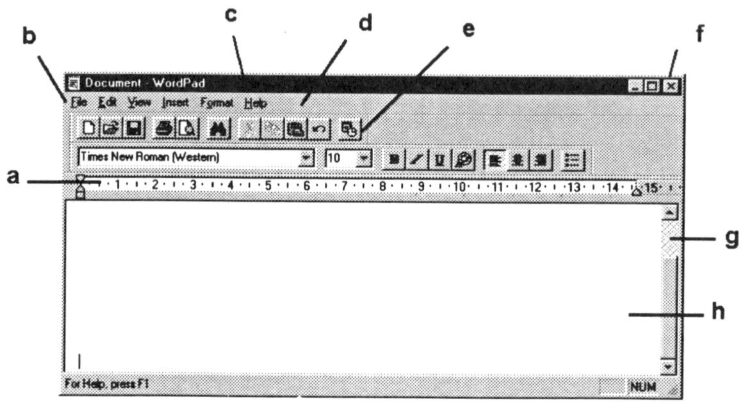

a. ______________________ e. ______________________

b. ______________________ f. ______________________

c. ______________________ g. ______________________

d. ______________________ h. ______________________

2. WordPad has lots of **icons** on its toolbar.
Each icon is a shortcut to a menu command.
What does each mean? Just leave the mouse pointer over them for a few seconds and their name will pop up!
Decide what each of these icons does and circle the best answer.

a.		Date / Time	Clock	Circle
b.		Binoculars	Find	Bottles
c.		Paper	Curly corner	New
d.		Open	Close	Folder
e.		Waste paper	Print	Robot
f.		Floppy disk	TV	Save

Saving your Work

Writing on paper stays there until you rub it out.
Typing in a word processor disappears when you turn the computer off.
To keep your typing for another time, you have to save it.
Your saved typing is called a document (or file).

To save a document in WordPad

Start WordPad. Type in the sentence 'Pewta likes seals.'

1. Click **File** on the menu bar.
2. Click **Save**.
3. Type in a useful name for your document. Call this one seal.
4. Click **Save.**

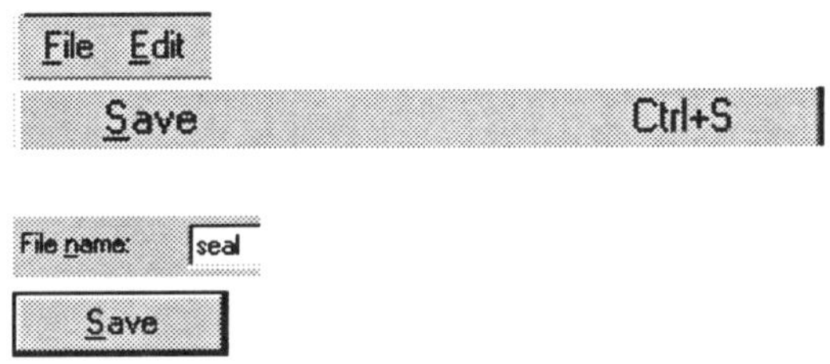

Questions

1. It's a good idea to save your document with a useful file name.
A useful file name tells you about what's in the document.
Look at this list of Pewta's WordPad files.
Which have useful file names?

a. **letter to aunt ceedee**	useful ☐	not useful ☐
b. **story**	useful ☐	not useful ☐
c. **pewta**	useful ☐	not useful ☐
d. **the rainbow day**	useful ☐	not useful ☐
e. **untitled**	useful ☐	not useful ☐
f. **my shopping list**	useful ☐	not useful ☐

2. It's a good idea to save your work every now and then as you are doing it.
Don't just save when you're finished. If the computer stops or if you make a big mistake, you could lose all your work!

- Pewta says you should save every single minute.
- Mouse-bot says save every ten minutes.
- Floppy-bot says to save just once an hour.

Whose advice will you follow? ____________________________

Opening your Documents

If you've saved a document, you can open it again.

To open a WordPad document

1. Start **WordPad**.
2. Click **File** on the menu bar.
3. Click **Open**...
4. Find the file name in the window.
   This time, find seal.
   Click the name.
5. Click the **Open** button.

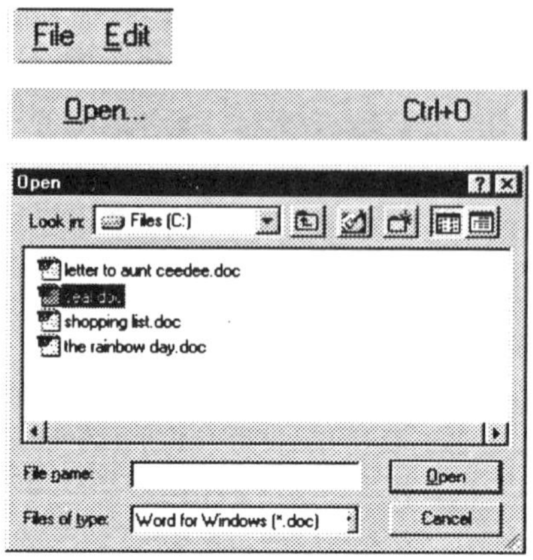

To open a recent WordPad document

1. Click **File** on the menu bar.
2. Click the document in the list.

Questions

1 seal.doc
2 shopping list.doc
3 letter to aunt ceedee.doc
4 the rainbow day.doc

WordPad remembers the **last four** documents you saved.

This is the list on Pewta's computer.

Did you see all the document names had the letter **.doc** after them? WordPad put doc (which is short for 'document') there. Windows now knows what kind of file they are.

1. What story has Pewta just finished working on? ______________________

2. What did she type before her seal story? ______________________

3. Who did she write to? ______________________

4. If Pewta saves a new story, which document will go off her list?

____

Printing

When you print, the program sends instructions to your printer. The printer changes the dots that make the words on your screen into dots of ink.

- Make sure it's okay to print before you start.
- Don't forget to turn on the printer
- Don't forget to put paper in!
- Use old scrap paper wherever you can.

Your turn

Make a number pattern to print out from WordPad.

- Type the number 1. Press **Enter**.
- Type in two 2s. Press **Enter**.
- Continue until you get to nine 9s.
- Now type in eight 8s again.
- Continue until you get back to one 1.
- It should look like the pattern on the right.
- Repeat again until you have two or three triangle patterns.
- Save your pattern. (See page 22 for help.)

1
22
333
4444
55555
666666
7777777
88888888
999999999
88888888
7777777
666666
55555
4444
333
22
1

To print a document

1. Click **File** on the menu bar.
2. Click **Print**...
3. Click the **OK** button in the Print dialog box.

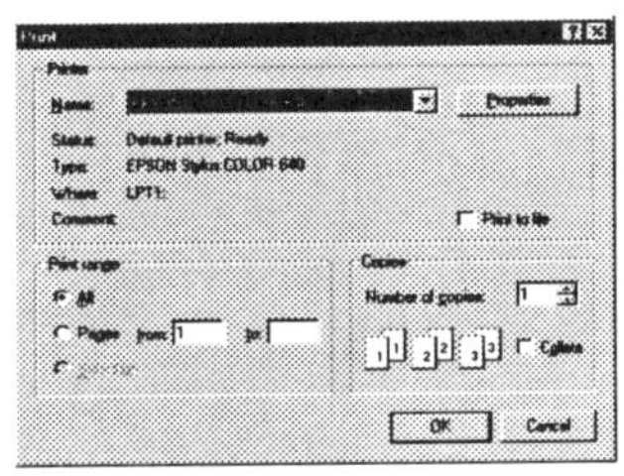

You can also print by clicking the Printer icon on the toolbar.

I like letters better than numbers. Can you make a letter pattern with one 'a' then two 'b's, three 'c's, all the way up to 26 'z's?

Fonts

Here are three 'sale' signs.

Sale Sale Sale

They all have the same word but the letters in each are written differently. They are in different **fonts**. WordPad makes it easy to change how your letters look.

Font size

Fonts come in different sizes.
Font size is measured in **points**.

Sale	Sale	Sale
10 points	**24 points**	**36 points**

Your Turn

Start WordPad and type in the words **'mouse-bot likes cheese'**.
It's a little small to see properly because WordPad starts off with a 10 point font.
To make it larger, select the text, then change its size.

To select the text

1. Click just to the left of the first word but keep the button pressed.
2. Drag to the end of the last word.
3. Release the left button.

To change the font size

Mouse-bot likes to eat cheese

1. Click the Font Size menu arrow.
2. Click a new font size.

Questions

1. What size font is each of these? (Circle the best answer.)

a.	b.	c.
Mouse-bot	Mouse-bot	Mouse-bot likes to eat cheese.
10 24 48	10 24 48	10 24 48

Font Families

Fonts also come in different families.

Sale	Sale	*Sale*
Arial	Times New Roman	Brush

To change the font family

1. Select the text.
2. Click the **Font** box arrow.
3. Click a new font family (such as Arial).

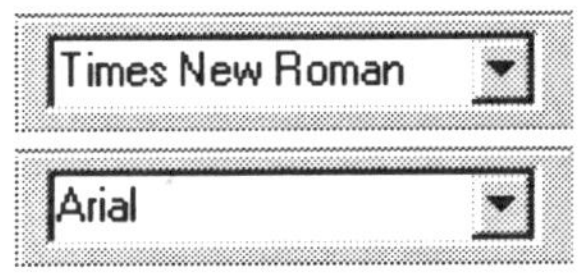

Questions

1. What font is each of these written in? (Write an answer.)

   a. *The quick brown fox* ____________________

   b. The quick brown fox ____________________

   c. The quick brown fox ____________________

   d. ❄♒♏ ❑◆♓♍& ____________________

   (Hint: the last font begins with 'wing'.)

2. Look at the list of fonts in WordPad.
   Write the names of five interesting fonts in the space below.

   a. __________________________

   b. __________________________

   c. __________________________

   d. __________________________

   e. __________________________

Font Styles

Fonts also come in different styles.

Sale	*Sale*	**Sale**
regular	italic	bold

WordPad usually starts off a regular font. Let's try changing the style.
Type in the words 'Mouse-bot likes cheese'.

To change the font style to bold

1. Select the text.
2. Click **Bold**. **B**

To change the style to italic

1. Select the text.
2. Click **Italic**. *I*

Questions

1. What style is each of these written in? (Write an answer.)

   a. **The quick brown fox.** ______________________

   b. *The quick brown fox.* ______________________

   c. The quick brown fox. ______________________

   d. *The quick brown fox.* ______________________

   e. ***The quick brown fox.*** ______________________ (Two styles!)

2. There are two more icons to change how a font looks.
   How does each change the text? (Write an answer.)

   a. Select some text and click U.

   ____

   b. With the text still selected click .

   ____

Alignment (1)

In WordPad you can change how the words you type line up. They can line up:

On the left	In the centre	On the right
These words are lined up on the left.	But these words are lined up in the centre.	While all of these words are lined up on the right.

Questions

1. Look at the names in these boxes.
   Are they lined up on the left, right or in the centre? (Circle an answer.)

Pewta	a.	Left	centre	right
Mouse-bot	b.	left	centre	right
Aunt Ceedee	c.	left	centre	right
Floppy-bot	d.	left	centre	right
Uncle Rom	e.	left	centre	right

2. WordPad uses three icons to align your text.
   Label them **left**, **centre** and **right**.

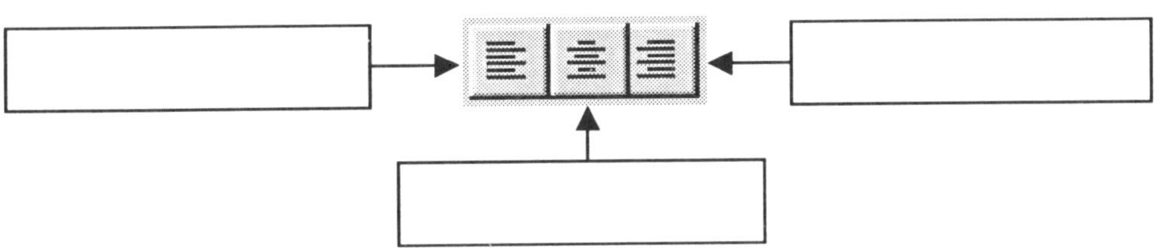

Your Turn

Centring is useful for headings. Let's type Pewta's name in WordPad and centre it.

1. Type Pewta.
2. Click anywhere in the text.
3. Click **Centre**. 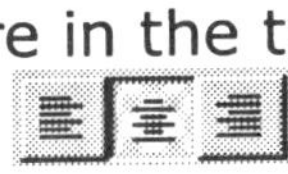

Alignment (2)

To right align your text

1. Click anywhere in the text.
2. Click **Right**. 

To left align your text

1. Click anywhere in the text.
2. Click **Left**. 

Questions

1. Write the names in the boxes with the correct alignment:

   a. Write **Floppy-bot** left aligned.

   b. Write **Mouse-bot** right aligned

   c. Write **Pewta** centre aligned.

2. What alignment do these buttons show?

   a. 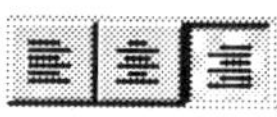 ____________ b. 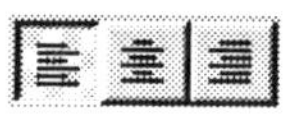 ____________ c. 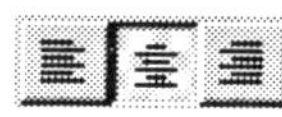 ____________

Your Turn

- Copy the text below into WordPad.
- Align each line correctly (look at the buttons for extra clues).
- Change the title to bold.

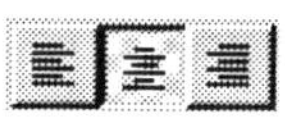

How to cross a road

Look right.

Look left.

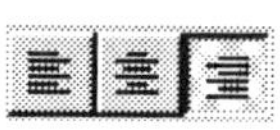

Look right again.

If all is clear, cross.

Page 2 — Meet the Guys

1. seal 2. cheese 3. dictionary

Unit 1: Your Computer

Page 3 — What Box is What?

1. a. printer b. keyboard c. speakers d. monitor e. system box f. mouse
2. a. speakers b. monitor c. keyboard d. system box e. printer

Page 4 — Buttons, Buttons Everywhere

1. Varied answers.
2. a. arrow keys b. backspace key c. mouse buttons d. Windows key e. shirt button f. monitor button

Page 5 — CD-ROMs and Floppy Disks

1. a. CD-ROM b. floppy disk
2. a. CD-ROM b. floppy disk c. both d. floppy disk e. CD-ROM f. floppy disk
3. Varied answers

Page 6 — Taking Care of Your Disks

1. Tick: a, b, e and g
2. a. disk b. closed c. magnets d. hot

Page 7 — Keeping Safe and Healthy

1. a. computer b. computer c. computer d. computer e. me f. me
2. a. rule a b. rule b c. rule c d. rule c

Page 8 — Let's get Started...

Varied answers.

Page 9 — Let's get Finished

1. a. 3 b. 1 c. 2
2. a. 3 b. 2 c. 1

Page 10 — The Desktop

Teacher to check.

Page 11 — Mouse Skills (1)

1. a. Mouse-bot b. real mouse c. computer mouse
2. Varied answers.
3. a. up b. down c. left d. right

Page 12 — Mouse Skills (2)

1. Teacher to check.
2. a. left b. right c. left d. right
3. Teacher to check.

Page 13 — Mouse Skills (3)

1. a. left b. twice c. drag d. right
2. a. The My Computer icon changes colour. b. The My Computer icon moves. c. A small menu appears. d. The My Computer program starts.

Page 14 — What's on the Menu?

1. f, a, e, b, c, d
2. Varied answers.

Page 15 — Opening and Closing Programs

Varied answers.

Page 16 — The Paint Screen

1. a. title bar b. menu bar c. close button d. vertical scroll bar e. horizontal scroll bar f. tool bar

Page 17 — The WordPad Screen

1. a. title bar b. menu bar c. close button d. vertical scroll bar
   e. horizontal scroll bar f. tool bar
2. a. a menu drops down b. the window changes size c. The pointer changes to I

Unit 2: Being Responsible

Page 18 — Taking Turns

1. Varied answers.
2. Varied answers.
3. Varied answers.
4. a. Unfair. Because Pewta has more time than the others.
   b. Varied answers.

Page 19 — Caring for Yourself

1. No
2. b. (two hours)
3. b. (take a break)
4. Feet on desk, typing one-handed, CD-ROMs left lying around.

Page 20 — Who Owns What?

1. a. fair b. hard c. copying d. pretending
2. a. Yes b. Ask Pewta first c. No
3. Yes
4. Varied answers.
5. Tim Tuck

Unit 3: Word Processing

Page 21 — Welcome to WordPad

1. Varied answers
2. Letters to the left are deleted.
3. A new line is started.

Page 22 — What's Where in WordPad

1. a. ruler b. file menu c. title bar d. menu bar e. tool bar f. close button
   g. vertical scroll bar h. document window
2. Circle: a. Date / Time b. Find c. New d. Open e. Print f. Save

Page 23 — Saving your Work

1. a. useful b. not useful c. not useful d. useful e. not useful f. useful
2. Mouse-bot's advice is best.

Page 24 — Opening your Documents

1. seal.doc
2. shopping list.doc
3. Aunt Ceedee
4. the rainbow day

Page 26 — Fonts

1. a. 24 b. 48 c. 10

Page 27 — Font Families

1. a. Brush b. Arial c. Times New Roman d. Wingdings
2. Varied answers

Page 28 — Font Styles

1. a. bold b. italic c. regular (or normal) d. italic e. bold and italic
2. a. Underlines the text b. Changes the text colour

Page 29 — Alignment (1)

1. a. left b. centre c. right d. centre e. right
2. left centre right

Page 30 — Alignment (2)

2. a. right b. left c. centre

Unit 4: Keyboarding

Page 34 — Check your Posture

1. a. poor b. good c. poor d. poor

Page 36 — Getting to Know your Keys (2)

1 a. 1 **2 3 4 5** 6 b. 5 **6 7 8 9** 0 c. Q **W E R T** Y d. T **Y U I O** P
e. A **S D F G** H f. F **G H J K** L g. Z **X C V B** N h. X **C V B N** M

Page 38 — Upper and Lower Case Letters

2. a. Adelaide b. Brisbane c. Canberra d. Darwin
e. Hobart f. Melbourne g. Perth h. Sydney

Page 39 — Using the Space Bar

2. **I** would like a seal for my birthday. **M**y seal would play with me.

My seal's name would be **H**oward the seal. **H**e would be my best friend.

Page 42 — Home Row Keys (3)

1. The **home** row is the row of keys your **hands** rest over when you type. Your **left** pointer finger rests over the F key. Your **right** pointer finger rests over the **J** key.
2. A S D (left) and K L ; (right)

Page 43 — Home Row Keys (4)

1. **A S D** F **G H** J **K L :**
2. 

Page 44 — Punctuation 1: Full Stops and Commas

1. a. **Sentences** begin with a capital or upper case letter.
b. People's names begin with a **capital** or upper case letter.
c. Place names begin with a capital or **upper case** letter.
d. Type a space **between** each word.
e. Type a **comma** between each item in a list.
f. Type one space **after** a full stop.
2. As per student's keyboard.

Page 45 — Punctuation 2: Question Marks and Exclamation Marks

1. a. 3 b. 1 c. 0 d. 1

Unit 5: The Internet

Page 50 — The World Wide Web

1. a. Sesame Street
2. a. Arthur! b. Coloring 4 Kids c. Hi-5 d. Playschool

Page 51 — Email

1. a. Aunt Ceedee b. Pewta's birthday present
2. 1 3 2 5 4

Page 52 — Welcome to Internet Explorer

1. a. 2 b. 1 c. 5 d. 4 e. 3 f. 7 g. 6
2. a. takes you back one page b. takes you forward one page
   c. takes you to the home page d. stops the page loading

Page 53 — Web Page Addresses

1. a. family b. school c. web page d. shop

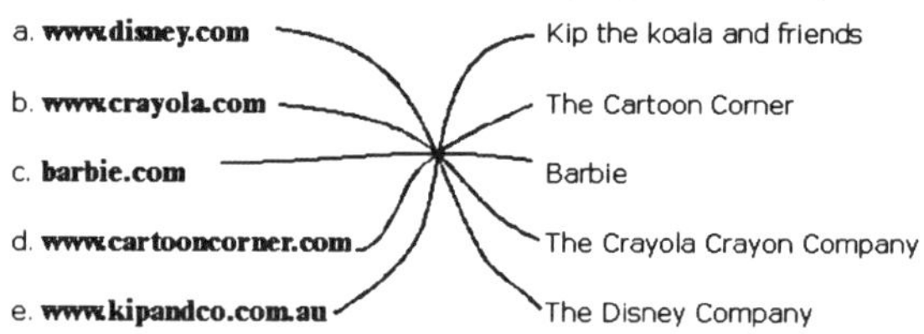

2.

Page 54 — What's on a Web Page?

1. a. 1 b. 2 c. 6 d. 7 e. 4 f. 5 g. 3
2. a. (www.zooatlanta.org)

Page 55 — Visiting Web Pages

1.
2. b. (www.adelaide-zoo.com.au)

Page 56 — Project: Scavenger Hunt

1. fur 2. sanctuary or zoo 3. On the ice 4. 1 – 1.5m 5. seals, sea lions and walruses
6. 4 2 5 3 1

Unit 6: Graphics

Page 57 — Welcome to Paint

1. a. title bar b. menu bar c. tools d. palette e. close button f. vertical scroll bar
   g. drawing area h. horizontal scroll bar
2. a. Select b. Fill With Color c. Magnifier d. Brush e. Text

Page 58 — Paint Tools: Brush

1. a. square b. backward slash c. circle d. forward slash

Page 60 — Paint Tools: Text

1. the text (or word) 2. the text (or word) 3. the text (or word)

Page 61 — Paint Tools: Shapes

b, c, e, and f

Project 1: A Picnic Poster

Here's a poster inviting people to a picnic.
Use your word processing skills to make your own poster in WordPad.

Instructions

- Fill in the blank spaces in the poster.
- Type all the text into WordPad, line by line.
- Change the font families, sizes and styles.
- Change the text alignment.
- Save your document. Call it **'picnic poster'**.
- Print out your poster.

Write the kind of picnic here.

Alignment	Font	
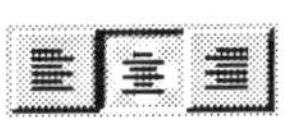	Arial 48 **B**	**SPECIAL _____ PICNIC**
	Arial 24 regular	There will be a special picnic on ____________ of next week. Everybody is welcome Bring a big plate of __________ Be ready for fun and games
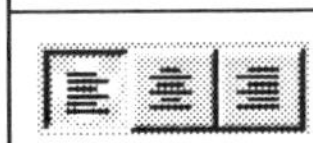		We start at __________
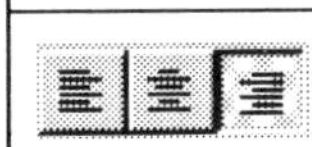		PS Bring a friend

Write the day here.

Write a kind of food to bring.

Write the time here.

When you've printed it out, add some pictures of picnic food and decorations!

Project 2: A Letter

This is a letter saying 'thank-you' for a present.
Can you make your copy in WordPad look the same as this one?

Instructions

- Fill in the blank spaces in the letter. Choose your own names.
- Type all the text into WordPad, line by line.
- Change the font sizes and styles.
- Change the text alignment.
- Save your letter. Call it **'Thank you letter'**.
- Print out your letter.

Alignment	Font	
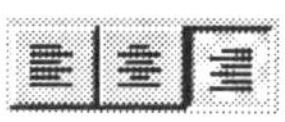	Arial 18 Regular	Mouse-bot Mouse hole 3 Pewta's kitchen
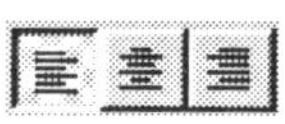	Was it a birthday of Christmas present?	Grandma Mouse-bot The house next door ________________ (Write the day here.) Dear Grandma, Thank you Grandma very much for my ____________ present. I've never had a _____________ before so I was very excited to get it. (Type the present here.) Thank you again,
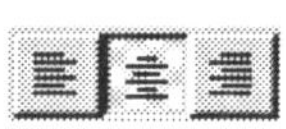	Arial 18 	*Love Mouse-bot*

Project 3: An Acrostic Poem

The first letters of each line in an acrostic poem spell out a word. Whose name does this poem spell out?

Pretty seal.
Everyone loves your
Wonderful
Tail and
Amazing tricks.

Instructions

- Write your name in the small squares. Write one letter in each box.
- Write a line starting with each letter of your name.
- Copy the poem into WordPad.
- Make the first letter of each line bold
- Save your poem. Call it **'acrostic poem'**.
- Print out your poem.

Check your Posture

It's important you're sitting and typing properly at the computer. Have a friend watch you and ask them to tick yes or no to each of the questions below. Use a pencil so you can take the posture test again!

Posture is another way of saying the way you sit and hold your body. **Good posture** helps you breathe correctly and feel comfortable. **Poor posture** can hurt your body.

Checklist for posture

1. Are you seated straight in front of the keyboard? Yes ☐ No ☐
2. Are both your feet on the floor? Yes ☐ No ☐
3. Are your elbows hanging comfortably at your sides? Yes ☐ No ☐
4. Are your fingers resting gently on the keyboard? Yes ☐ No ☐

Checklist for finger position

1. Are your fingers resting gently on the keyboard? Yes ☐ No ☐
2. Are you keeping your fingers curved and upright? Yes ☐ No ☐
3. Are you pressing the keys lightly? Yes ☐ No ☐
4. Are you using both hands to type with? Yes ☐ No ☐

Questions

1. Look at these pictures of Pewta typing.
   Write the word **good** if she has good posture or finger position.
   Write the word **poor** if she has poor posture or finger position.

a.	b.	c.	d.

Getting to Know your Keys (1)

Knowing where all the keys are on your keyboard is important.
The faster you find them, the quicker you can type.

Questions

On the keyboard below:

1. Colour the letters A, S, D, F, G, H, J, K and L red.
2. Colour the other letter keys blue.
3. Colour the number keys yellow.

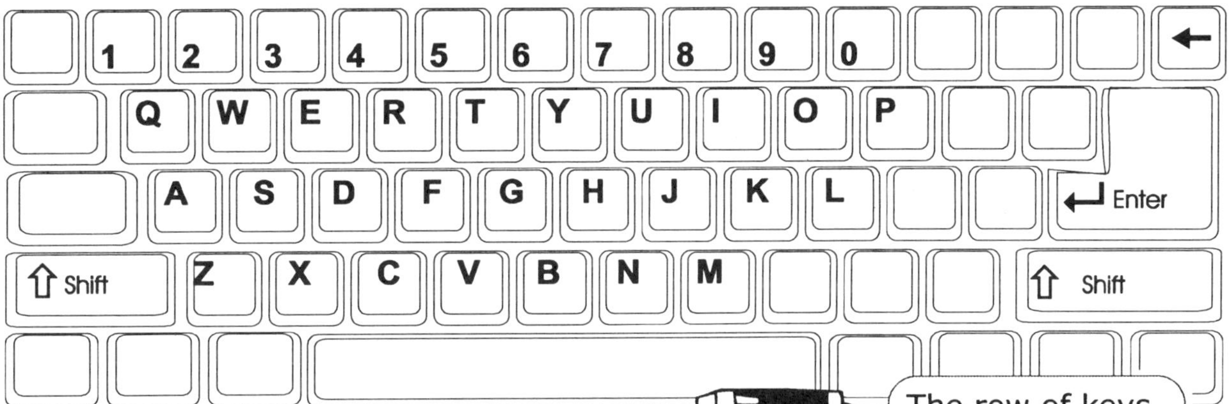

On the keyboard below:

4. Colour the Backspace key green.
5. Colour the Enter key brown.
6. Colour the Shift keys purple.
7. Colour the space bar orange.

Getting to Know your Keys (2)

Questions

1. Whoops! Below are some strips of keys from a keyboard but the letters are rubbed off!

   Write in the missing letters and numbers.
   Colour in the F and J keys red whenever you write them.
   Use this keyboard to help.

a. 1 _ _ _ _ 6

b. 5 _ _ _ _ 0

c. Q _ _ _ _ Y

d. T _ _ _ _ P

e. A _ _ _ _ H

f. F _ _ _ _ L

g. Z _ _ _ _ N

h. X _ _ _ _ M

Entering Text

It's time to type some text patterns!

Your Turn

- Start WordPad.
- Click the **Font Size** arrow. Click 24. (So you can see the type more easily.)
- Type each pattern.
- Tick each one as you complete it.
- Save your document as **'patterns 1'**.
- Print out your document when you finish.

Patterns 1–4

1. 11 22 33 44 55 66 77 88 99 00 ☐ done!
2. qq ww ee rr tt yy uu ii oo pp ☐ done!
3. aa ss dd ff gg hh jj kk ll ☐ done!
4. zz xx cc vv bb nn mm ☐ done!

Patterns 5–8

5. 11 00 22 99 33 88 44 77 55 66 ☐ done!
6. qq pp ww oo ee ii rr uu tt yy ☐ done!
7. aa ll ss kk dd jj ff hh gg ☐ done!
8. zz mm xx nn cc bb vv ☐ done!

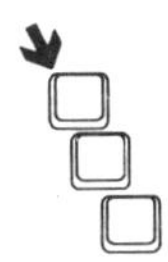

Patterns 9–10

9. qaz wsx edc rfv tgb yhn ujm ☐ done!
10. zaq xsw cde vfr bgt nhy mju ☐ done!

Upper and Lower Case Letters

Upper case letters look like this: A B C D E. (They're are also called capitals.)
Lower case letter look this: a b c d e

To type upper case letters using the Shift key

1. Press and hold down the Shift key (don't let go yet!).
2. Press a letter key.
3. Take your finger off the Shift key.

Questions

1. Label this keyboard picture with lower case letters.
   Colour in the Shift keys green. Colour the Caps Lock key blue.

2. Here's a list of Australian capital cities but each capital needs a capital letter!
   Rewrite them in the space with an upper case first letter.

a. adelaide
b. brisbane
c. canberra
d. darwin
e. hobart
f. melbourne
g. perth
h. sydney

Your Turn

1. Type the capital city list into WordPad.
2. Use the Shift key to make the first letter upper case.
3. Press Enter after each city.
4. Save your document as **'capital cities'**.

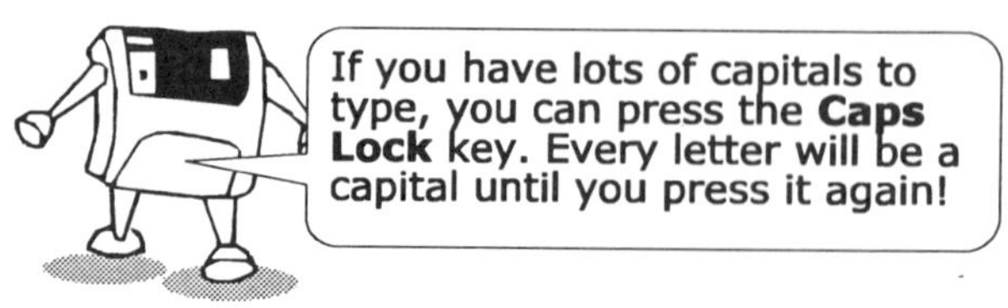

Using the Space Bar

When you are typing:

Do	Don't
• Put a space in between words. • Use your right thumb to tap the space bar. • Put one space after a full stop.	• Put lots of extra spaces between words. • Use spaces to start a new line. Press the Enter key instead.

Questions

1. Colour the long space bar blue.
   Colour the Shift keys green and the Caps Lock key blue.

2. Read Pewta's story below and correct her mistakes.
   Change sentence beginnings and names to upper case letters.
   Circle any places where Pewta has pressed the space bar too much.

i would like a seal   for my birthday.   my seal would play with me.

my seal's name   would be howard the seal. he would   be my best friend.

Your Turn

1. Type Pewta's story into WordPad.

2. Type these patterns of letters into WordPad.

   a. A B C D E F G H ... S T U V W X Y Z (Hint: use CAPS LOCK.)

   b. AA BB CC DD EE ... VV WW XX YY ZZ

   c. Ssssh Ssssh Ssssh Ssssh Ssssh Ssssh (Hint: use the SHIFT key.)

   d. oooOooo oooOooo oooOooo oooOooo

Home Row Keys 1

Some people can type without looking at the keyboard. Because their fingers can find the keys without looking, they can type quickly.

Home for your fingers and feet

Try walking around your room without looking.
Check your feet out. Where do they go when you stop?
The floor is like a home for your feet.
The floor (or ground) is where your feet go when they're not busy.

The middle row of keys on the keyboard ASDFGHJKL;) is called the **home row**.
The home row is where your fingers go when they're not busy.

Questions

1. Colour the home row red.

2. Your two pointer fingers are important when you type.
Connect the dots on the drawing to complete the pointer fingers.
Colour in the nails on the pointer fingers red.

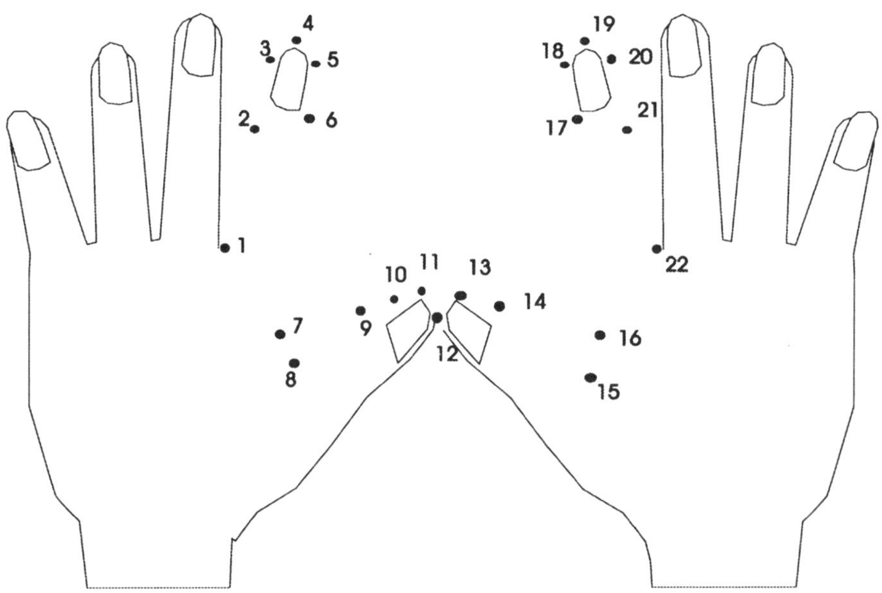

Home Row Keys (2)

Find the **F** and **J** keys on your computer keyboard. If you look closely you may find a little bump on each key. F and J are where your two pointer fingers rest.

Your Turn

Read all the instructions first.

- Close your eyes and gently move your fingers over the keyboard.
- Stop when you find the bumps.
- Place your left pointer finger on the left bump.
- Place your right pointer finger on the right bump.
- Open your eyes.

Now try again but find the two bumps more quickly.

Here are some practice exercises for your two pointer fingers.
- Try to type *without* looking at the keyboard.
- Use one of your thumbs to press the space bar in between.
- Type each pattern five times.
- Write a two pointer finger exercise in the space below. Try it in WordPad.

1. jjjj ffff jjjj ffff jjjj
2. jj ff jj ff jj ff jj ff
3. jfjf jfjf jfjf jfjf jfjf
4. jjff jjff jjff jjff jjff

Questions

Colour the pointer fingernails and the F and J keys red.

Home Row Keys (3)

Questions

1. Fill in the missing words.

   Use these words: | home left right hands J |

   The ______________ row is the row of keys your ______________rest over when you type. Your ______________pointer finger rests over the F key. Your ______________pointer finger rests over the ______________ key.

2. With your pointer fingers over F and J, where will your other fingers be? Complete this picture with the correct keys.

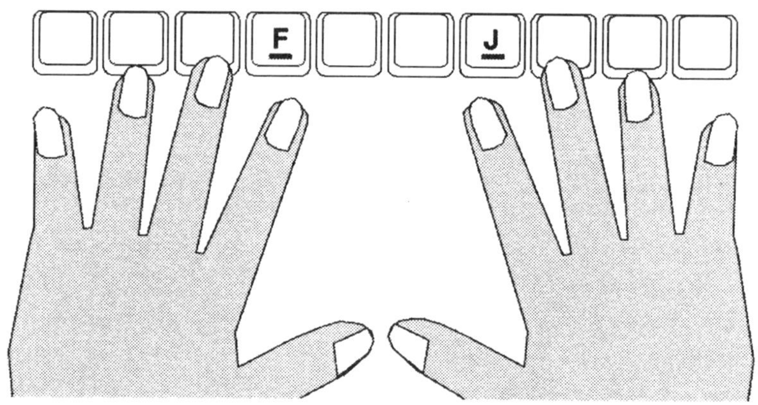

Your Turn

More exercise for your fingers!

- Try to type *without* looking at the keyboard.
- Use one of your thumbs to press the space bar in between.
- Use your right hand little finger to press the Enter key after each line.
- Type each pattern five times.
- Make sure you use the correct fingers.

Left hand

1. aaaa ssss dddd ffff
2. asdf asdf asdf asdf
3. as as as as as as as
4. df df df df df df df

Right hand

5. jjjj kkkk llll ;;;;
6. jkl; jkl; jkl; jkl;
7. jk jk jk jk jk jk jk
8. l; l; l; l; l; l; l; l;

Home Row Keys (4)

Questions

1. Write the home row keys on this picture. Try not to look at the keyboard.

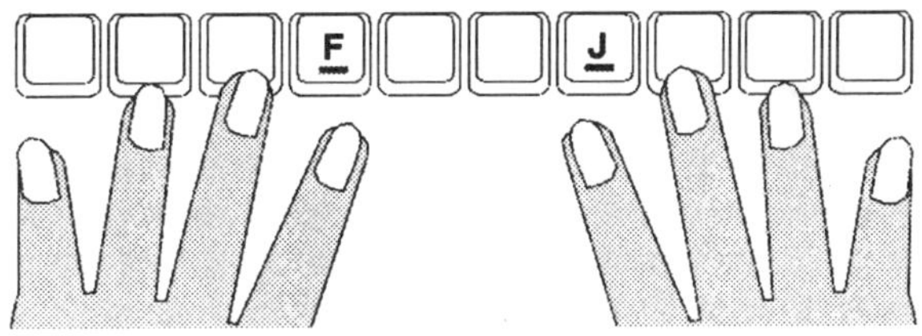

2. Your right hand little finger rests on the key next to 'L'. Draw this key here. The top symbol is a colon. The bottom symbol is a semicolon.

Your Turn

Try typing the following letters, words and sentences into WordPad.

Both hands together

1. aajj aajj aajj aajj
2. sskk sskk sskk sskk
3. ddll ddll ddll ddll
4. ff;; ff;; ff;; ff;; ff;;
5. asdf jkl; asdf jkl;
6. alsk alsk alsk alsk
7. dfjk dfjk dfjk dfjk
8. fjas fjas fjas fjas
9. ha ha ha ha ha ha

Real words (tricky!)

10. ask ask ask ask ask
11. ash ash ash ash ash
12. sad sad sad sad
13. lad lad lad lad
14. flag flag flag flag
15. gash gash gash gash
16. dash dash dash
17. flash flash flash flash
18. flags flags flags

And to finish—two whole sentences!

19. a sad lad had half a flag
20. a glad gal has flash daks

Punctuation 1: Full Stops and Commas

Full stops are used to end sentences.
Commas are used to separate items in a list.

Questions

1. Use these words to complete the sentences below.

Sentences	capital	upper case	comma	between	after

   a. ________________ begin with a capital or upper case letter.

   b. People's names begin with a ________________ or upper case letter.

   c. Place names begin with a capital or ________________ letter.

   d. Type a space ________________ each word.

   e. Type a ________________ between each item in a list.

   f. Type one space ________________ a full stop.

2. The keyboard has keys for each different punctuation mark.
   Find each of these punctuation marks on your keyboard.
   Write them in the correct place on the blank keyboard below.

!	,	.	?

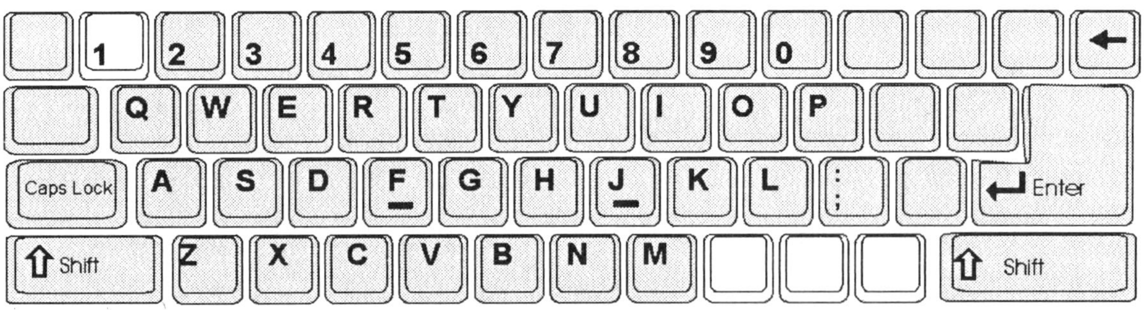

Your Turn

Start WordPad and type these sentences. Type a space after each comma.

1. Pewta likes seals, mice and ducks.
2. Mouse-bot likes cheese, carrots and fudge.
3. Floppy-bot likes his disk box.

Punctuation 2: Question Marks and Exclamation Marks

? Question marks show that a questions is being asked.

To type a question mark:

1. Hold down the left shift key with your left hand.
2. Tap the question mark key with your right hand.

! Exclamation marks show that something exciting is happening.

To type an exclamation mark:

1. Hold down the right shift key with your right hand.
2. Tap the exclamation mark key with your left hand.

Questions

Read the poem.

A hen ate the fruit from a tree.
Her tummy felt awful, she sat in the shade.
The hen's baby chicks cried with glee.
Come look at the orange mamma laid!

1. How many full stops are there? ________
2. How many commas are there? ________
3. How many question marks are there? ________
4. How many exclamation marks are there? ________

Your Turn

1. Start WordPad and type these sentences.

   a. Have you washed your hands?
   b. Is there a seal in the garden?
   c. Where is Mouse-bot hiding?
   d. Look out for the falling fudge tin!
   e. Your picture is fantastic!
   f. Those scissors are sharp!

2. Type the poem above into WordPad and centre each line.

Project 1: An Alphabet Chart

Classroom often have charts to help children remember the alphabet.
Here's one that Floppy-bot started:

A is for apple
B is for bitmap
C is for computer
D is for disk
E is for electricity
F is for floppy disk

Make your own alphabet chart in WordPad.

Your Turn

- Start WordPad.
- Change the **font size** to 18.
- Type a capital letter A then the words 'is for'. Press **Enter**.
- Type a capital letter B, then the words 'is for'. Press **Enter**.
- Continue with each letter of the alphabet up to Z.
- **Save** your document as 'alphabet chart'.
- It should look like this:

A is for
B is for
C is for
D is for

- Left click just after the word 'for' on the 'A' line.
- Press the **space bar** then type a word beginning with A.
- Left click just after the word 'for' on the 'B' line.
- Press the **space bar** then type a word beginning with B.
- Continue with each line up to Z.
- **Save** again and **print**.

Project 2: Font Sampler

Make a sampler of your favourite font.
Tick each instruction as you complete it.

ooXooXooX ooXooXooX ooXooXooX ooXooXooX

Font Sampler

0123456789
abcdefghijklm
nopqrstuvwxyz

ABCDEFGHIJKLM
NOPQRSTUVWXYZ

ooXooXooX ooXooXooX ooXooXooX ooXooXooX

Your Turn

Step 1: Type in the top border and title

- Start WordPad and **Centre** the first line. ☐
- Type in a pattern of letters across the top to make a border. ☐
  You could type something like this: **ooXooXooXooXooXooXoo**
- Press the Enter key four times (to leave some space). ☐
- Type in the title 'Font Sampler'. Press Enter twice. ☐
- **Save as** **'font sampler'**. ☐

Step 2: Type in the alphabet and numbers

- Type the numbers from 1–9. Press Enter twice. ☐
- Type the lower case letters from a–m. Press Enter. ☐
- Type the lower case letters from n–z. Press Enter four times. ☐
- Type the upper case letters from A–M. Press Enter. ☐
- Type the upper case letters from N–Z. Press Enter four times. ☐
- Type in a pattern of letters across the bottom to make a border. ☐
- **Save** your document. ☐

Step 3: Change the font families and sizes

- Select the title. Change to 36 point size. ☐
- Select the numbers and four lines of letters. ☐
- Change to 36 points and your favourite font. ☐
- **Save** and **print**. ☐

Project 3: A Pangram

The five boxing wizards jump quickly.

a b c d e f g h i j k l m n o p q r s t u v w x y z

Cross off each letter of the alphabet as you find it in the sentence above. What do you notice? That's right, it has every letter of the alphabet in it! Here's another pangram.

The quick brown fox jumps over the lazy dog.

Let's turn it into an Alphabet Sampler.

Your Turn

- Start WordPad and **Centre** the first line. ☐
- Type in the alphabet in lower case as a top border. ☐
- Press the Enter key four times.
- Type in each word of the sentence. Press the Enter key after each word. ☐
- Press the Enter key four more times. ☐
- Type in the alphabet in lower case as a bottom border. ☐
- Select the words. Change to 36 point size and an interesting font. ☐
- **Save** as **'pangram'** and print. ☐

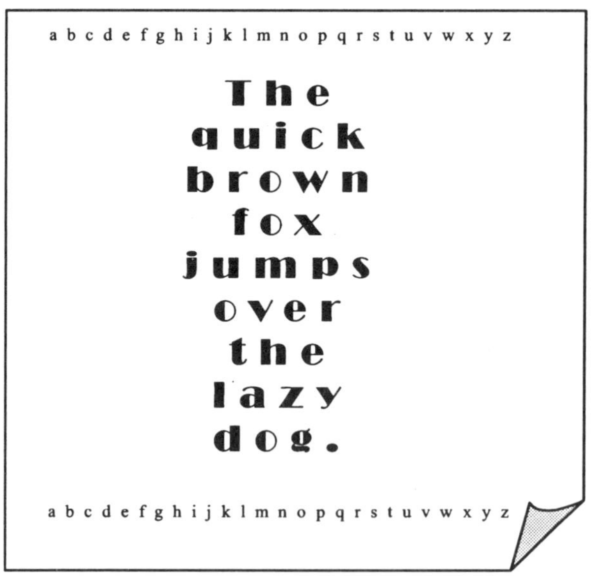
a b c d e f g h i j k l m n o p q r s t u v w x y z

The
quick
brown
fox
jumps
over
the
lazy
dog.

a b c d e f g h i j k l m n o p q r s t u v w x y z

Welcome to the Internet

Computer networks

Floppy-bot has connected Pewta's computer to her parents' computers.

Now they can share documents, the printer and the telephone line.

Floppy-bot says the three computers are joined together like the string in a net. He calls it a computer **network**.

Pewta's home network

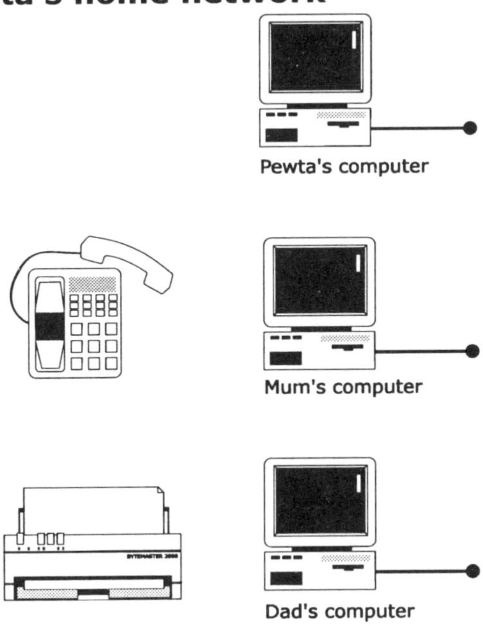

The Internet: A bigger network

The Internet is also a network of computers. But it has millions of computers joined together using telephone lines, cables and satellites.

Computers on the Internet can play games together, send each other email and share pictures, music and information.

The Internet

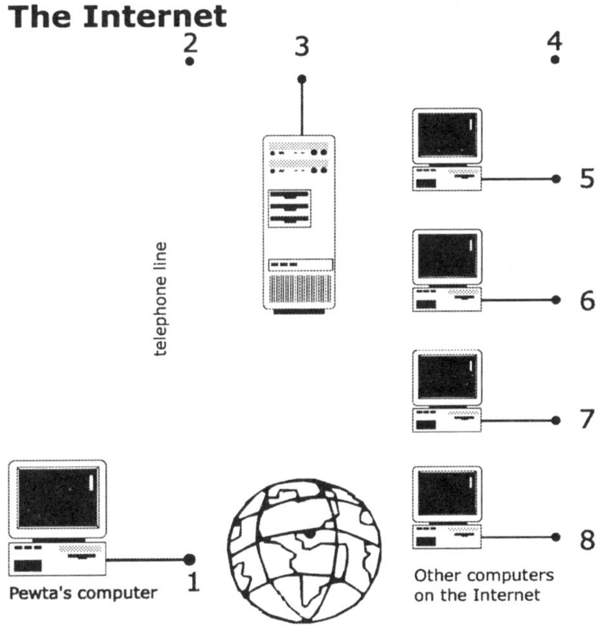

Questions

1. On Pewta's home network picture:
   a. Connect the three computers together.
   b. Connect the telephone to Mum's computer.
   c. Connect the printer to Dad's computer.

2. On the Internet diagram:
   a. Connect Pewta's computer to the Internet company (join 1, 2 and 3).
   b. Connect the Internet company to the other computers on the Internet (join 4-8).

The World Wide Web

Most of the pictures, music and information are on the part of the Internet called the World Wide Web. You use a program called a browser to find and view them. The Windows browser is called **Internet Explorer**.

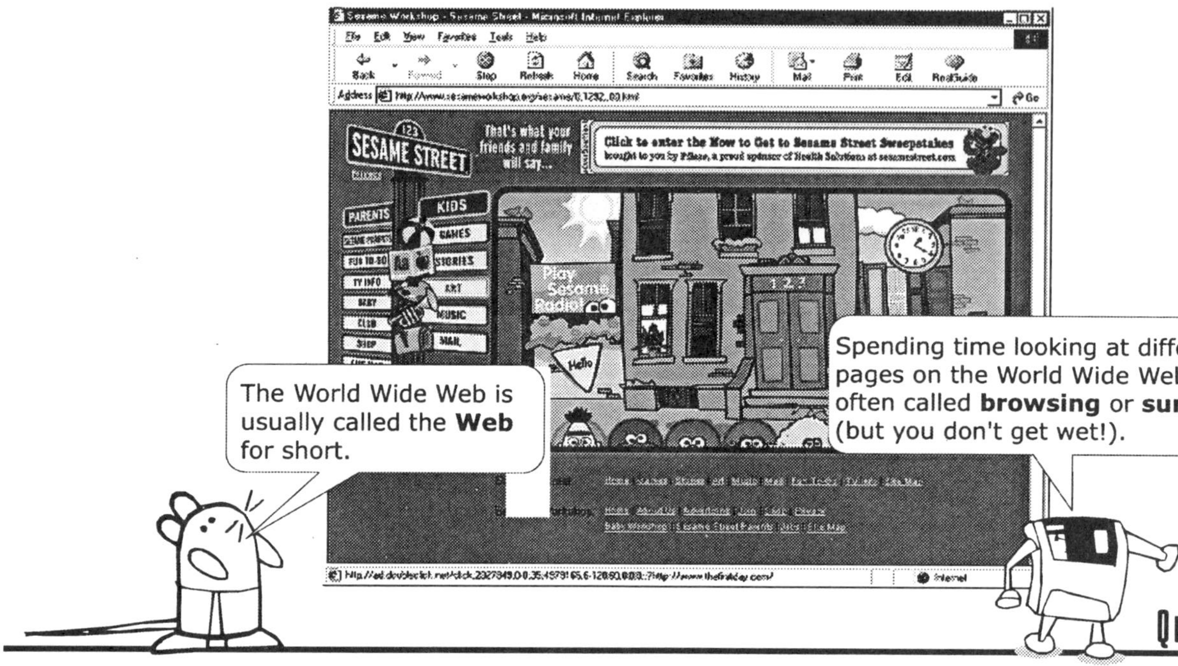

Questions

1. Look at Pewta's Internet Explorer program above.
   a. Write the name of the page she's looking at. ____________________
   b. Circle the **Close** button. (Hint: look in the top right hand corner.)
   c. Colour the **menu** bar red.
   d. Colour the **toolbar** blue.

2. Pewta's been browsing the World Wide Web.
   She visited Coloring 4 Kids, Arthur, Hi-5 and Playschool.
   Write the names of the pages she visited below their pictures.

pbskids.org/arthur/

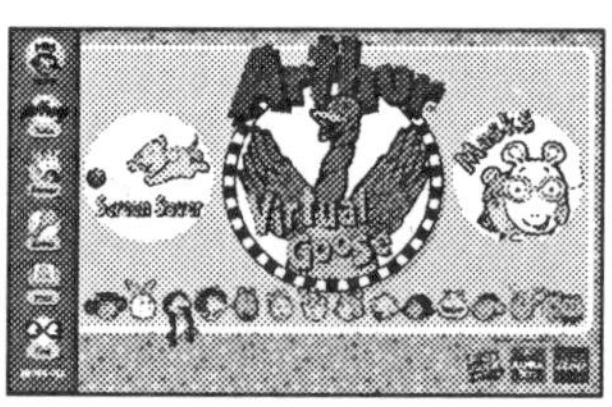

a. ____________________

www.coloringpage.org/

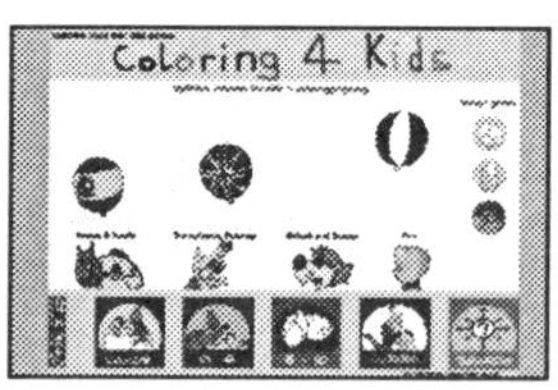

b. ____________________

ninemsn.com.au/kids/hi5/

c. ____________________

www.abc.net.au/children/play/

d. ____________________

Email

You can send messages to other people on the Internet.

To send and receive email you need an email program. The Windows email program is called **Outlook Express**.

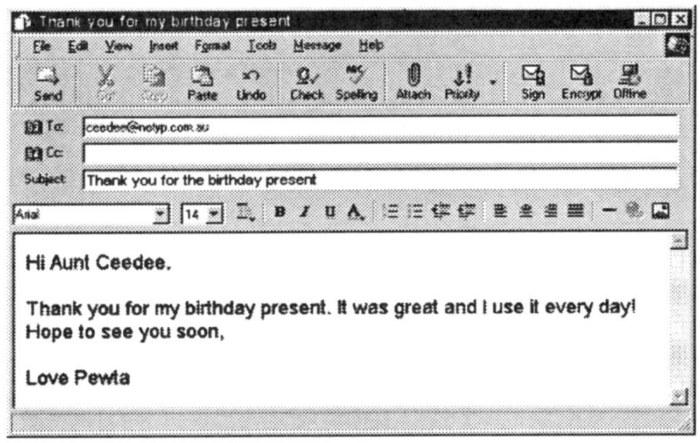

Questions

1. Answer these questions about Pewta's email message.

   a. Who is Pewta writing to? ______________________________

   b. What is her message about? ______________________________

   c. Circle the Send button.

2. Read the sentences below. They explain how Pewta sends the email message to her Aunt Ceedee—but they're in the wrong order.
   Write the numbers from 1–5 in the boxes to show their proper order.
   Use the pictures for help

☐ Pewta starts her email program.
☐ She clicks the Send button.
☐ She types her message.
☐ The email is stored on a computer Aunt Ceedee can connect to.
☐ Pewta's email program connects to the Internet and sends the email.

1

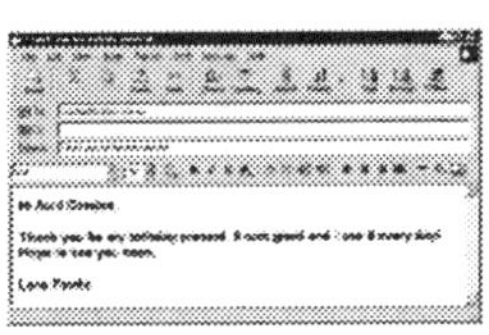
2

3

4

5

Welcome to Internet Explorer

To start Internet Explorer

1. Click the **Start** button.
2. Point at **Programs**.
3. Click **Internet Explorer**. 

Questions

1. Write a number in each box to match the arrows to the list words.

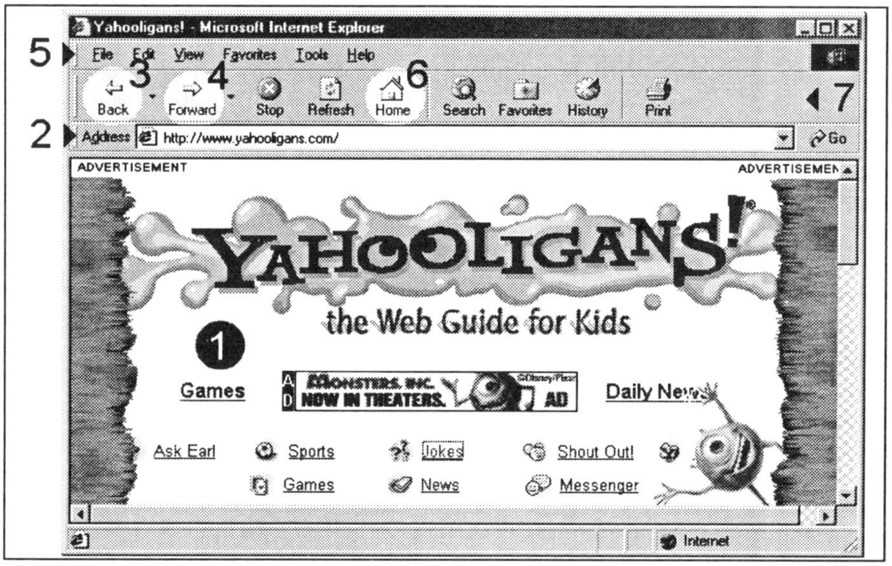

a. ☐ Address bar
b. ☐ Yahooligans! page
c. ☐ Menu bar
d. ☐ Forward button
e. ☐ Back button
f. ☐ Toolbar
g. ☐ Home button

2. What does each of these Internet Explorer buttons do?
Choose the best answer from the list and tick the box.

a. 

makes the page face backward ☐ takes you back one page ☐

b. 

makes the page face forward ☐ takes you forward one page ☐

c. 

takes you to the home page ☐ shows you your home ☐

d. 

stops the page loading ☐ stops you using the browser ☐

Web Page Addresses

Families, schools and shops have addresses. Web pages also have addresses.

Yahooligans! is a website for children. It has lots of information about interesting web pages to visit. This is the Yahooligans! web address.

www.yahooligans.com

Questions

1. Decide who these addresses belong to.
   There's a shop, a family, a school and a web page.
   Write your answer beneath each address.

Mr and Mrs Morris 23 Robert St Oldtown NSW	Arthurton Area School Box 23 Arthurton SA	www.yahooligans.com	Fred's Flowers 91 Commercial Rd Allensbury QLD
a.	b.	c.	d.

2. Join these home page addresses to their companies using lines.

a. **www.disney.com**	Kip the koala and friends
b. **www.crayola.com**	The Cartoon Corner
c. **barbie.com**	Barbie
d. **www.cartooncorner.com**	The Crayola Crayon Company
e. **www.kipandco.com.au**	The Disney Company

What's on a Web Page?

Here's the home page for the Atlanta Zoo.

Questions

1. Write a number in the box to show where you would click:

   a. For visitors' information. ☐

   b. For the zoo calendar. ☐

   c. To see panda photographs. ☐

   d. To visit the kids' pages. ☐

   e. To buy raffle tickets. ☐

   f. To search for information. ☐

   g. For more pages to visit. ☐

2. Here are three addresses. Which one do you think is the Atlanta Zoo home web page address? Tick the box.

   a. **www.zooatlanta.org** ☐

   b. **www.thisistheatlantazoohomepage.org** ☐

   c. **Atlanta Zoo, 235 Zoo Drive, Atlanta USA** ☐

Visiting Web Pages

To visit a new web page

1. Click in the address bar.

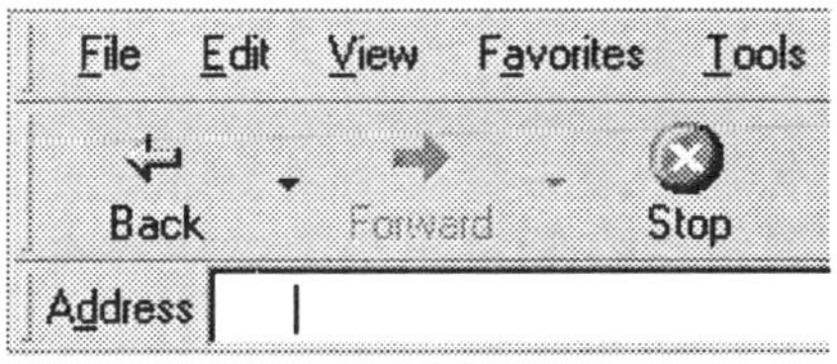

2. Type in the address.

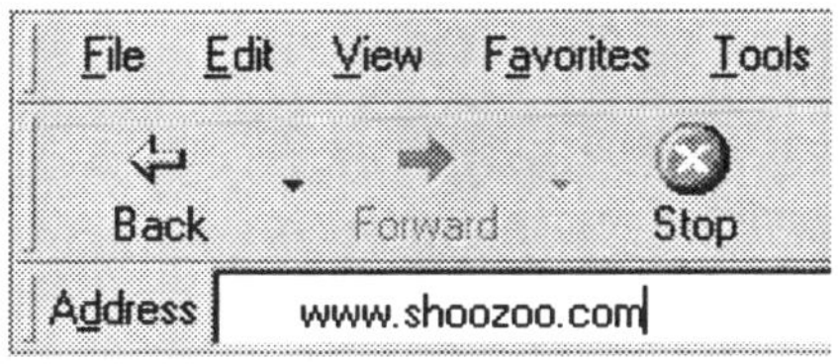

3. Press the Enter key.

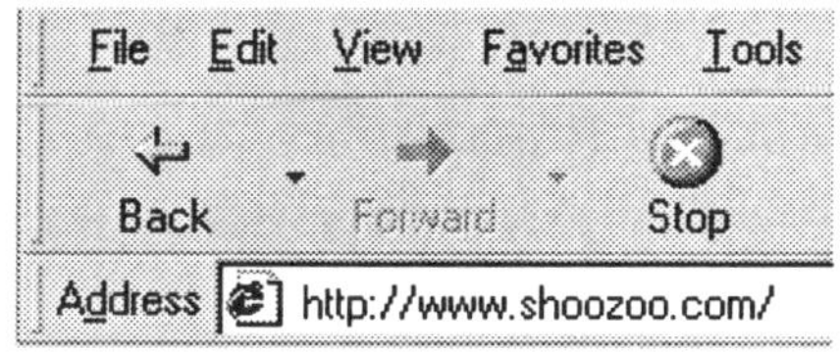

It's important to type the web address in exactly right. If you:

- miss out a letter or spell a word wrong
- put in a space
- muddle the upper case and lower case letters

your browser won't be able to find the page for you.

Questions

1. Type the web addresses into the address bar on your browser. Use a line to join the correct address to the picture.

a. www.perthzoo.wa.gov.au b. www.adelaide-zoo.com.au c. www.mogozoo.com.au

2. Pewta was trying to visit the Adelaide Zoo page. Which one do you think is the correct address? Tick the box.

a. WWW.ADELAIDE-ZOO.COM.AU ☐

b. www.adelaide-zoo.com.au ☐

c. www.adelaidezoo.com.au ☐

d. wwwadelaidezoocomau ☐

e. www.Adelaide Zoo.com.au ☐

Hint: look at the addresses on this page.

Project: Scavenger Hunt

Pewta's made a scavenger hunt for you!

She visited five web pages and found information about seals. Visit each page and write an answer for each question. Remember to type in the web page address exactly, or your browser won't find it.

Questions

1. www.earthwindow.com/mammals.html
   The Guadalupe ______________ seal has a long name.
2. www.sealsanctuary.co.uk/bas4.html
   Where are these seals living? ______________
3. www.photolib.noaa.gov/animals/seals1.html
   These seals might be cold. Why? ______________
4. collections.ic.gc.ca/arctic/species/harbour.htm
   How long is a Harbour Seal? ______________
5. www.pinnipeds.org/
   What three animals does this organisation help protect?
   a. ______________ b. ______________ c. ______________
6. Match up these pictures to the websites. Write a number in each box.

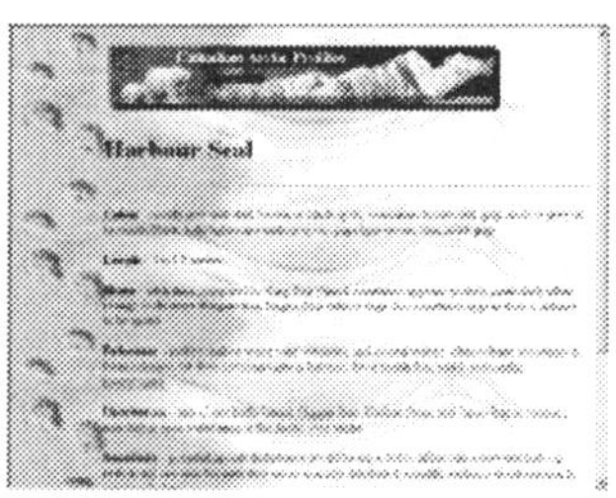

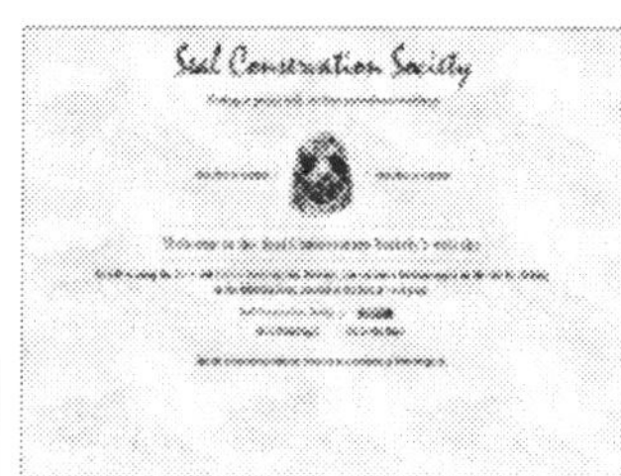

Welcome to Paint

'Graphics' means pictures and designs. You can use the Windows' graphic program **Paint** to create your own pictures and designs.

To start Paint

1. Click **Start**.
2. Point the mouse at **Programs**.
3. Point to **Accessories**.
4. Click **Paint**. 

Questions

2. Label the sections of the Paint screen below. Use these words.

tools, title bar, menu bar, vertical scroll bar, palette horizontal scroll bar, close button, painting area

a. ______
b. ______
c. ______
d. ______

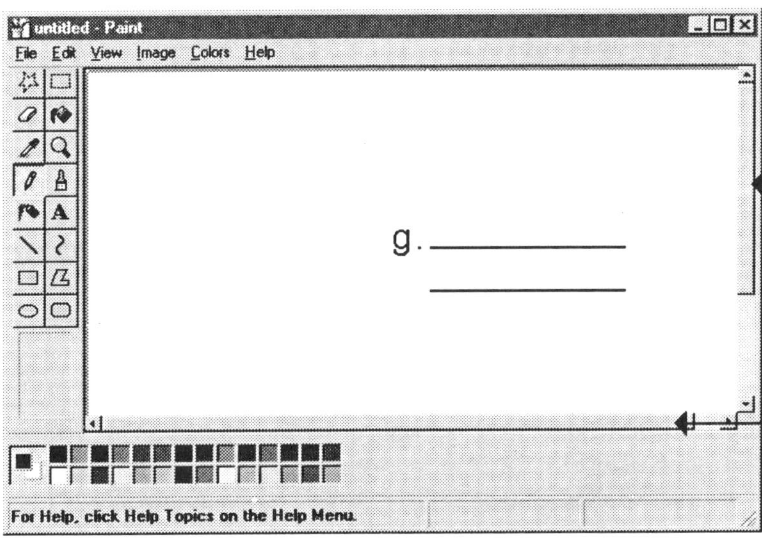

e. ______
f. ______
g. ______
h. ______

3. Here are some of Paint's tools. Five are named. Label the others.

Free form select tool
Eraser / colour eraser
Colour picker
Pencil
Airbrush

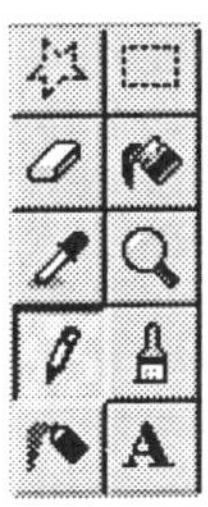

a. ______
b. ______
c. ______
d. ______
e. ______

Paint Tools: Brush

You'd expect a program called Paint to have a paintbrush. Paint's paintbrush can change shape, size and colour. There's no messy brush to wash afterwards either!

To paint with the brush tool

1. Click on the brush icon.
2. Point the mouse at the drawing area. The pointer changes to a cross–hair.
3. Click and drag the crosshairs around the drawing area.
4. Release the mouse button to stop.

Paint has four brush shapes. Each shape comes in 3 sizes.

Circle	Square	Forward slash	Backward slash
●	■	/	\

To change the brush shape

- Click on a brush shape beneath the tool box.

To rub out mistakes

1. Click on the eraser icon.
4. Click and drag across your mistake.

Questions

1. Which brush shape did Pewta use to draw these four lines?

a.	b.	c.	d.

Your Turn

1. Paint these shapes:

Square	Circle	Loops	dots

5. Create a rectangles picture

- Draw a rectangle around your page.
- Draw a smaller rectangle inside it.
- Draw a smaller rectangle inside that one.
- Can you guess what to do next?
- Keep drawing rectangles until you run out of room.

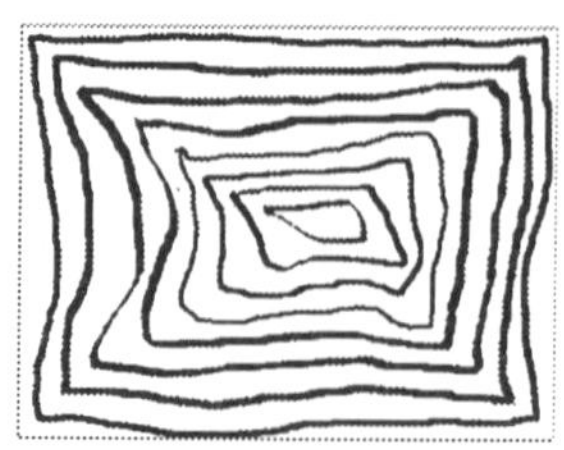

Paint Tools: Pencil

The pencil tool doesn't *look* very exciting. In fact, when you first use it, you might think it's just a skinny brush. But the pencil has a trick up its sleeve...

To draw with the pencil tool

1. Click on the pencil icon.
2. Point the mouse at the drawing area. The pointer changes to a pencil.
3. Click and drag the pencil around the page.
4. Release the mouse button to stop.

The invisible ruler

Try this trick and discover the invisible ruler!

1. Click on the pencil icon and move the mouse into the drawing area.
2. Hold down your Shift key on the keyboard.
3. Click and drag the mouse across the screen. Release the mouse button.

The two-colour pencil

Let's add an extra colour to your Paint pencil.

1. Click red in the palette.
2. **Right-click** on blue in the palette.
3. To draw in red, click the **left** mouse button and drag in the drawing area.
4. To draw in blue, click the **right** mouse button and drag in the drawing area.

Your turn

Create a diagonals picture.

- Click on the pencil icon.
- Select a colour from the colour palette.
- Hold down the **Shift** key on the keyboard.
- Draw diagonal lines from left to right.
- Select a new colour.
- Hold down the **Shift** key on the keyboard.
- Draw diagonal lines from right to left.

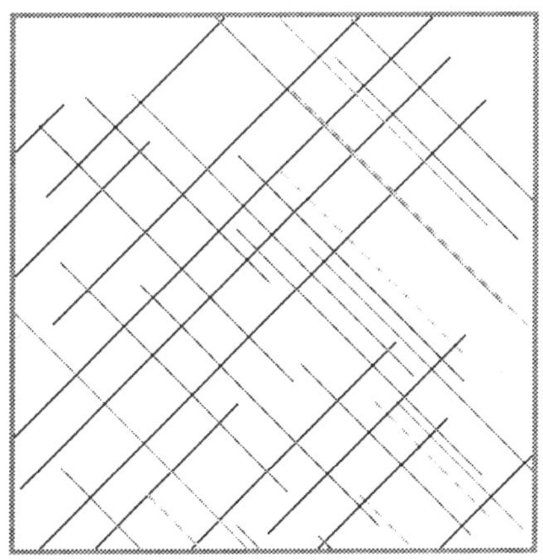

Paint Tools: Text

Use Paint's text tool to add titles, sentences or labels to your paintings.

To add text

1. Click the **Text** tool. A
2. Point the mouse at the drawing area. The pointer changes to a cross–hair.
3. Click and drag a box for your text.
4. Type into the text box.
5. Click outside the text box to finish.

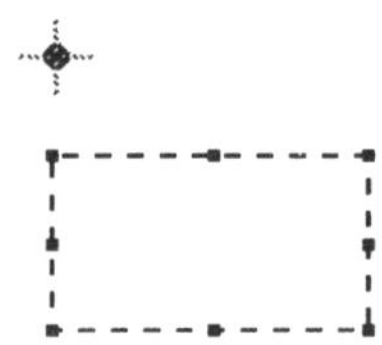

To change the text background colour

1. Right-click the new colour in the colour palette.
2. Click the **Text** tool.
3. Draw a text box for your text.

Questions

Create a text box and type your full name in the box.
Click the **View** menu and click **Text Toolbar**.
Write an answer to each question.

1. Click a new colour in the colour palette.
   What changes colour? ______________________
2. Click the Bold icon.
   What turns bold? ______________________
3. Click Font size. Click 48.
   What changes size? ______________________

Your turn

Create a set of school book labels.

- Right click light-grey in the colour palette.
- Click the **Text** tool icon.
- Click and drag a text box across the screen.
- Type in a school book name.
- Click **Bold** on the **Text Toolbar**.
- Start again for your next label.
- Print the labels out when you're finished.

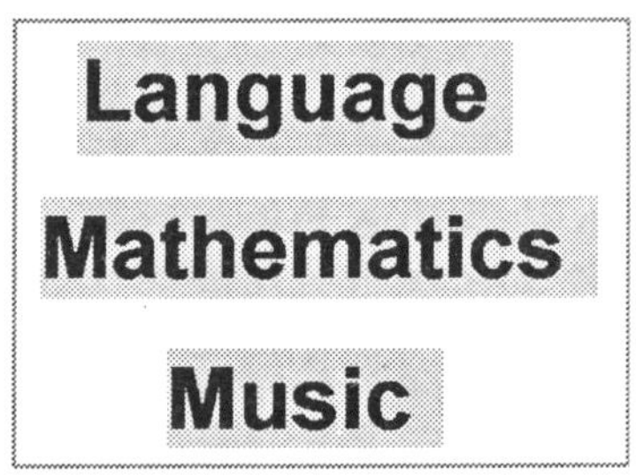

Paint Tools: Shapes

Paint has special tools for drawing shapes.

To draw a rectangle, rounded rectangle or oval

1. Click the rectangle rounded rectangle or oval (ellipse) tool.
2. Click and drag the shape.
3. Release the mouse button.

To draw a square

1. Click the rectangle tool.
2. Hold down the Shift key.
3. Click and drag the square.

To draw a circle

1. Click the oval (ellipse) tool.
2. Hold down the Shift key.
3. Click and drag the circle.

To draw a polygon (many-sided shape)

1. Click the Polygon (many-sided shape) tool.
2. Point at the drawing area.
3. Click and drag the first side.
4. Click to draw the next side.
5. Continue clicking for each new side.
6. Double click to finish the shape.

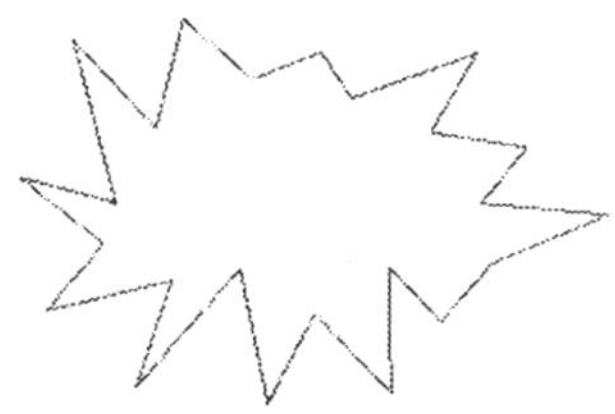

Questions

1. Look at these shapes. Colour those drawn with the Shift key held down.

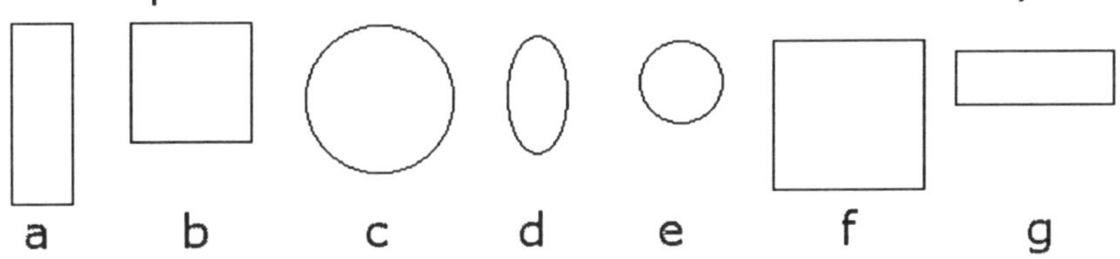

Your Turn

Make a surprise shape!

1. Click the Polygon tool .
2. Hold down the Shift key.
3. Draw a many sided shape.
4. Surprise surprise!

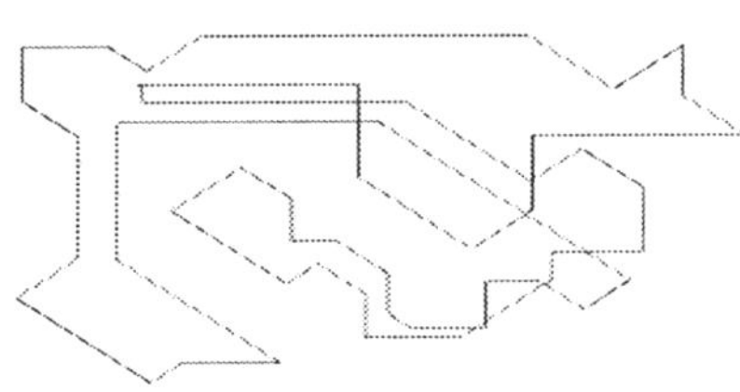

Paint Tools: Lines

Paint has two special tools for drawing lines

To draw a straight line

1. Click the **Line** tool.
2. Point at the drawing area.
3. Click and drag the line.
4. Release the mouse button.

To draw a curve

1. Click the **Curve** tool.
2. Point at the drawing area.
3. Click and drag a line.
4. Click to one side of the line. The line bends towards the click.
5. Click on the other side. The line bends towards the click.

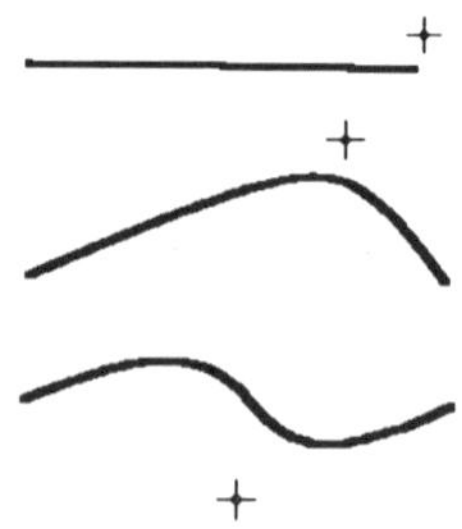

Your Turn

Create a landscape picture.

Step 1: Draw the hills

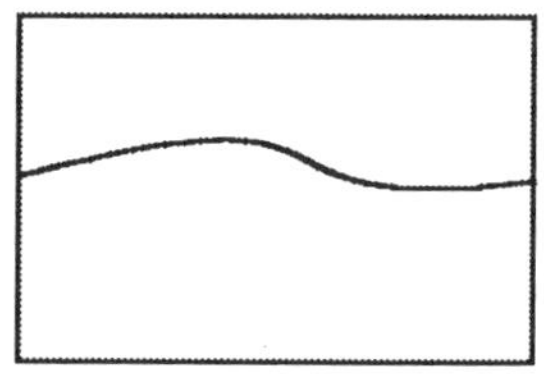

- Click the **Line** tool and click the thickest line.
- Click the **Rectangle** tool. Draw a rectangle border around your screen.
- Click the **Curve** tool.
- Click the border on the left and drag to the right side. Release the mouse button.
- Click *above* the line and drag up.
- Click *below* the line and drag down.

Step 2: Paint the grass and sky

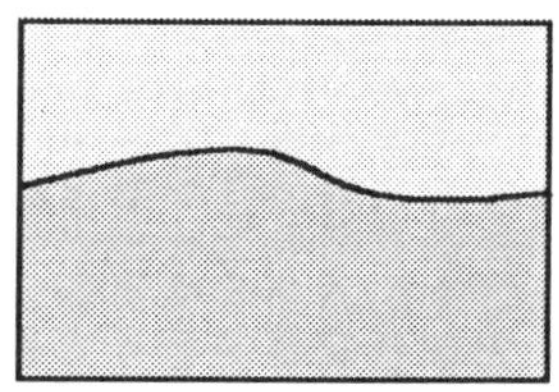

- Click the **Fill** tool.
- Click green. Click below the hills to paint them green.
- Click blue. Click above the hills to paint the sky.

Step 3: Add the sun

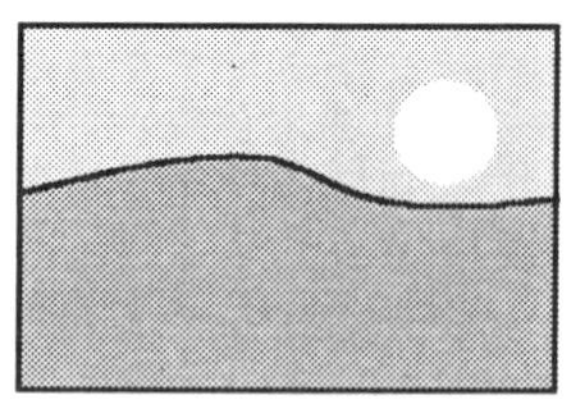

- Click on the **Ellipse** tool.
- Click the bottom shape below the toolbox.
- Right click on yellow.
- Hold the Shift key down and click and drag a sun above the hills.

Project: A Bedroom Door Sign

Make a sign for your bedroom door.

Step 1: Write your name

- Start Paint.
- Click the Text tool. 
- Click in the drawing area.
- Type in your name.
- Click the Fonts list. Click a new font. (Pewta used Arial.)
- Click the Size arrow. Change the point size to 72.
- If you can't see all your name, point your mouse at the bottom-right corner.
- Your mouse pointer changes to a double-headed arrow.
- Click and drag the corner until your whole name appears.
- Click outside of the text box.

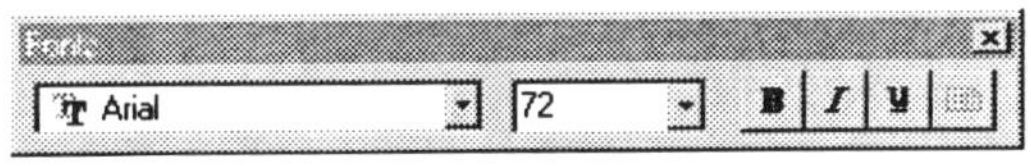

Step 2: The border

- Left-click the Brush tool.

- Choose a brush shape from the palette below.
(Pewta used the large square.)

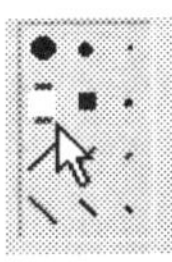

- Choose a colour from the colours palette.

- Click lots of dots around your name.

Step 3: Decorations

- Click the **Rectangle** tool. 
- Click a colour from the palette.
- Click and drag lots of small rectangles around your name.

Here is Pewta's finished sign.

Step 4: Save your door sign

- Click the **File** menu.
- Click **Save**.
- Type in a name for your door sign. (Pewta used the title 'my door sign'.)
- Click **OK**.

Step 5: Print your door sign

- Click the **File** menu.
- Click **Print**.
- Click **OK**.

Other things to try

- Use lots of different shapes instead of just rectangles.
- Experiment creating decorations using the  air-brush tool.
- Write your name on the sign in different colours.
- Fill in the letters of your name in different colours.